M000076915

FEEDBACK

"Groundbreaking and provocative. A fast, funny and informative read on sex, life and, yes—respect. An insight into the basic, fundamental elements of relationships…A modern look at how men and women interact."

—Brenna Hatami, Naturopathic Doctor and Yoga Teacher

"A woman dates 12 men over the course of a year in the name of science…Written in a chatty, brisk style, the book is most engaging when Kelton attempts to follow the "dating rules" offered by various self-help books…The chapter in which she orders pheromones from the Internet and enlists her friends as test subjects is especially amusing…A fun, intriguing premise."

—Kirkus Discoveries

"A hilariously honest and insightful look at modern dating, filled with fascinating information on the science of love… fabulous!"

—Mohini Moore, Creative Consultant

"Challenging other authors that are driven by their own dating rules Kelton courageously opens up her personal life delivering an original and refreshing perspective into the world of dating…entertaining and thought provoking…a must read that simplifies relationships!"

—Jack Teetor, Marketing Executive

"Finally! Someone who communicates! Honestly and truly…A first in your face "here's what's on my mind" book. No rules, no pretension, just life, real and raw…as it should be. Inspirational in every way."

—Valerya Gurevich

"A great view of dating from a woman's perspective…A REAL single girl's story of the wild and crazy dating world we live in today. Kelton freely tells of her experiences without fear of judgment. This book has changed every point of view and a certainty that I was having…This book is exactly what I needed. Thank you for sharing with me."

—Shanti Mari Kennedy

"A candid, clever and comedic look at love, lust and the thrill of the hunt. But what exactly are we hunting for? This book offers insight into the minds and motivations of men and women on the dating scene: and why we do what we do."

—Carrie Cash Brewer,
Photographer, Designer, Producer, Surfer

"Kelton's in your face take on human behavior is humorous, straightforward, insightful and filled with valuable observations…I became so engulfed while reading that it felt like I was watching a great movie always wanting to know what would happen next… A first-rate read that I will recommend especially to some of my guy friends…looking forward to part two!"

—Jonathan Pascual, Real Estate Investor

Don’t Use My Sweater Like a Towel

Don’t Use My Sweater Like a Towel

Jennifer Kelton

Don't Use My Sweater Like a Towel

Published by Green Knights Press
www.greenknightspress.com

Author's note: The events described in this book occured as related and in real time. Some names and identifying characteristics have been changed.

Green Knights Press
578 Washington Boulevard, Suite 388
Marina Del Rey, CA 90292
www.dontusemysweaterlikeatowel.com
Jennifer@dontusemysweaterlikeatowel.com

Book cover design by
Frank Rivera, Jolie O'Dell and Jennifer Kelton

Printed in the United States on recycled paper

Don't Use My Sweater Like a Towel
Jennifer Kelton

1. Title 2. Author 3. Nonfiction Self-Help/Relationships

Library of Congress Control Number: 2005927034
ISBN-10: 0-9790723-0-1
ISBN-13: 978-0-9790723-0-7

Dedicated to the human spirit
and its constant ability to evolve.

In memory of
R.C. (1965–2006)

Acknowledgements

My deepest gratitude to everyone along the path who shared with me your valuable input. Without your assistance, this book and journey would not have been possible.

Mom and Dad: Because of you, I am here. I am truly blessed with your endless love and support.

All my friends.

The test and survey subjects.

The 12 men.

All the bartenders who took care of me and supported my wine and food habits while using their bars as a second office:

Canal Club—Jose, Santigo, Shino, Edison, Chano, Luis.
Baja Cantina—Jim, Pete Kasper, Mike D.
Typhoon—Juan, Chad, John, Brian, Sammy, Ou, Anthony, Chris.
I Cugini—Bryan, Gregorio; Angel, you really are one; Jennifer D., you are a goddess, even when you sweat! A huge thanks to both of you for your help during my nights of frustration. I still think that the salmon and Caesar is better than the shrimp corn fritters for comfort food.

Chaya Venice—Dev, I promise (well, maybe) that the title of my next book will be *Dev*; Betsy, you rock! Better, stronger, wiser!
Mercedes Grill—Mike, I miss seeing you.
Crustacean—Raffy, you are the king! Nilo, "Hey sexy, yes my red pen is just to look important, you are a joy"; Mark sorry you never got to see the screen saver.
The Lobster—Dave, Mark, Leah (service with a smile); Dhyana, thanks for the input.
Mandarin Oriental—Olivia, Lisa, creating a memorable fortieth birthday. I felt like Alice in Wonderland—you're the best!
Jennifer: I look at the gift everyday on my desk—powerful! Thank you.
Everyone who generously and openly answered the survey questions.

Thank you to Victoria, Ashley, and Elise.

Leigh (for dealing with my perfectionist qualities): Yes, I can be a bear to work with.

Yoga teachers along the way: Heath, Jesse, Kimberly, Diane, Matthew, Erika.

The pheromone testers: Stella, Snowflake Alcaraz, Sophie, Danika, Taylor, Georgia, Giselle, Lily, Magadalena, Ruben, Chivers, Holmes, Jimmy Stingray.

Everyone at Miiamo: Genny, Kendra, Juan, Jay, Jeff, R.J.

HUGE thanks to the hundreds of random people who I have met along the way who gave me your honest thoughts and opinions of life.

Tom and Brett the two guys at the bar in Venice.

Perri: fellow hat girl—for planting even more seeds and encouraging me to write this book.

Carolina: for the Picasso.

Mary: your expert thoughts and experiences.

Peanut Lennon at Direct 2 Models: always great to talk with you at the bar.

Sharon: You rock! I will always look forward to fun and frolics at Fidel's.

Peer Review group: Steve, Anna, Brenda, Mom, Sharon and Valerya.

Jeff Posey—I will drive to Bishop on next big snow storm to get you a steamer.

Last but not least to the two bartenders Roy and Luke at the Four Seasons: Thanks for feeding me on New Year's Eve 2005. I'm glad I didn't have to bite your faces off!

Table of Contents

Disclaimer

The content of this book is not meant to be malicious or hurtful. All names have been changed to protect the innocent and not so innocent.

The opinions expressed in this book are solely those of Jennifer Kelton.

> *Who among us is an expert on the human experience? We have only the gift of sharing perceptions that hopefully can help those on their journey. There is no such thing as an expert on the human experience.*
>
> —Gary Zukav, *The Seat of the Soul*

Don’t Use My Sweater Like a Towel

Introduction

The meeting of two personalities
is like the contact of two chemical substances:
if there is any reaction, both are transformed
—Carl Jung

INTERSTATE 10 STRETCHES 2,460 miles from Santa Monica, California to Jacksonville, Florida. It is one of three coast-to-coast interstates that span the United States of America. The daily average traffic count in my hometown of Los Angeles is approximately 329,000 cars. Combine that with the other totals across the country and you have lots of traffic, lots of people and lots of life. Each day when you wake up, you never know exactly what will occur. Life and its assortment of circumstances are not always in your control. Nature, just like traffic, will do as it pleases.

During the summer, I saw a remarkable story on the morning news about a young boy who had survived a shark attack. In an extraordinary twist of fate, he knew what to do from watching a Discovery Channel show just the day before. During the family's interview, the young boy's mother said that because her son was still young "he sometimes gets caught up in the small stuff." She will then remind him that he fought off a shark, conveying to him what he has survived—of life's bigger picture.

Life gives us each our own shark to fight, often more than one. I am alive as a result of modern medicine, including five life-saving surgeries. Also thrown into the mix was an extremely serious car accident that left me unconscious for about a month when I was seventeen years old. These experiences make me feel incredibly lucky to be here on planet

Earth. I had to fight to be here, and like the boy who survived the shark attack, I fought hard.

When I was in my early thirties, I was told that modern medicine held no more remedies for me. With no real answers but many questions about my own existence, I had to face my newest life challenge openly. It was a difficult, intense time. Within a few years life lead me to the shamans of South America and Siberia, with whom I studied, trained and received advice. On that six-year road I had scores of life-changing experiences. It was the shamans' willingness to share their love, lives and insights that opened my mind and spirit, healing my body. They taught me the true meanings of humility, compassion and connection with the elements.

The ancient world of shamanistic healing and wisdom dates back to "the very horizons of our knowledge."[1] Its teachings brought me back into the modern world ready to face whatever lay ahead. I am better, stronger and wiser from my own shark fights; I work not to get bogged down with the small stuff—to keep my eye on the bigger picture.

A little over a year ago, I realized my two-year relationship was not fulfilling my needs. After a lot of thought and with a broken heart, I ended it in search of a more ideal fit. The fast lane of dating and singledom is filled with ups, downs and in-betweens, along with a huge range of emotions in every shade of gray. What started for me as a quest for love, companionship and a possible soul mate turned into a science project.

Now approaching forty years on this planet, never married and with no kids, I am back on the single-and-dating 10 Freeway, where you can get shot at, flipped off, tailgated and cut off. You can also have that rare moment when someone lets you make an easy lane change as you exchange genuine smiles.

I am out a lot, and I meet lots of people. Each man I encountered during my year of science represents a microcosm of behavior that everyone may recognize. Though you never know what is going on in someone else's thoughts, each of us has the ability to make good, constructive choices based on what we know in our own minds. When it comes to relationships, there are no strict rules to follow, no exactly "right" behaviors—much like the 10 at rush hour. It is important to stay alert, watch your back and make safe lane changes.

Each and every one of us seeks happiness and validation in some shape or form. Finding happiness in oneself is the first step to finding happiness with another. We learn the most from our own mistakes, as well as life's hardships and triumphs. On that road of self-discovery, among millions of drivers each day, it's nice to know we are not alone.

I have a motto that has evolved out of many years of running my own business: As long as you are honest, organized and on time, you will be fine. I live by these words. It is just that plain and simple. It's about keeping your word and being respectful of your fellow human beings.

This book is a raw, real, no-holds-barred look at dating, relationships, love and human nature in the twenty-first century. I have no advice (well, maybe a little), I only have experiences with plenty of spontaneous, punk-rock moments. These have been my most effective teachers.

My hope is that this book will plant the seeds of discovery that can enrich not only your relationships, but also your entire life. Perhaps you can glean something useful or maybe just have a good laugh. Read on—laugh, cry, feel frisky, be brave, be thoughtful—and learn a little about yourself and your fellow drivers out on Interstate 10.

Be warned: not for the underage or faint of heart! The following pages contain sexually graphic material. (And yes, my family may disown me!)

Chapter One

SIMON
The Ex-Boyfriend

February 2002–June 2004

IN JUNE 2004, I broke up with my boyfriend of two years. Simon and I had a deep emotional connection. Thankfully, to this day, we remain the best of friends. There were so many reasons to stay in the relationship. We laughed all the time; we share a taste for the finer things—great food, travel, clothing. Our lifestyles are still very compatible. He is kind and honest, with a true heart of gold. Unfortunately, these numerous good qualities could not make up for the bad—the things that I feel are crucial to a life of joy and happiness.

Simon is a talented film director, a self-confessed workaholic. At that time in his life, he was always preoccupied with his career. For many months, he had not been present with me. Right before our breakup, I went to Japan to visit him on location. I might as well have been in LA—it was that bad. He was extremely distant, barely noticing I was there. Sadly, I was having more fun on my own.

I did my very best to be sympathetic of his work situation; he was under enormous job pressure. It came as no surprise to me that he would be exceedingly busy with the film and baby-sitting its self-absorbed star. Demanding is not my style, but I had flown halfway around the world to spend time with him, so I expected some kind of acknowledgment. We also weren't having sex, my sheer nightgown not withstanding.

That was a huge problem. We hadn't had sex in four or five months, and he didn't touch me the whole time I was in Japan. As we would go to bed, Simon would mutter good night, quickly roll over and fall asleep. Maybe he just didn't like the nightgown.

The night before I left, we went out to dinner. I told him that things had to change when he got back to LA. Our relationship was draining me; it had lost its joy, and I was feeling very unfulfilled. I was always there for him, but he did not give me the same in return. There is a great quote in *He's Just Not That Into You*, by Greg Behrendt and Liz Tuccillo, that encapsulates how I felt: "Shitty relationships make you feel shitty and that is not what you were put on this earth for." I knew I deserved more and I was determined to get it.

When he returned, things remained pretty much the same. I could tell he was trying a little bit harder, attempting to do the best he could at the time. He showed up with flowers more often than not, but he was still preoccupied. It was all about Simon, and then more about Simon. I knew his selfishness was unintentional. He was not trying to be mean, it was just him. It was his life, and I was not a part of it.

I needed some time to think, away from the hustle and bustle of the LA lifestyle. Using some frequent flyer miles, I booked myself a flight to Oahu for the weekend. I confess to having somewhat of an addiction to the Mandarin Oriental hotels. Feeling extravagant, I booked a room; I would be a glamorous woman for the weekend.

Though it was June, it did not occur to me when I made my reservation that the resort would be saturated with brides and grooms upon my arrival. Everywhere I turned there was a rehearsal dinner, a wedding, a wedding reception or a honeymooning couple. Since it was summer, there were also an unbelievable number of families with kids on holiday. It seemed that I was the only single woman guest at the hotel.

Confident in my own independence, I felt lucky to be there. Even in the midst of the traditional romantic trappings, I enjoyed myself. There was never a moment when I felt lonely, unloved or unlovable. I soaked up the warm Hawaiian sun and the glow of my hard-won self-assuredness.

After a day spent by the ocean—an early morning workout and sunning, followed by a massage in the spa—I sat at the bar, completely relaxed. In a sarong and flip-flops, I overlooked the landscape of coupledom, marriagedom and familydom amongst the palms and plumeria flowers. I thought to myself, *Simon and I are not going to go there.* After too long in a sexless, one-sided relationship, I knew it was over. Oddly, I felt good. There was sadness*, but on the flip side of the coin was relief.*

The trade winds blew as the Hawaiian sun just started to dip below the horizon. With a cocktail in hand, I bravely dialed Simon's number on my cell. I broke up with him right there at the Mandarin Oriental bar, watching the couples old and new, with visions of what could be.

The decision to end our relationship, though somewhat spontaneous and definitely the right thing, was not an easy one. I was plagued with the questions we all have before the inevitable breakup: Will I meet someone else?

Will I find that "ideal" relationship? Will my neighbors investigate the stench coming from next door when they realize I haven't been seen in weeks? Will my family hear about my lonely death on the 5:00 news and be even more surprised to hear that I adopted stray cats when I've always been a dog person?

After a bit of searching, I realized: yes, yes, no and no.

Even if I never meet "the one," I will never be alone. People surround me. I am lucky to have the most amazing, unconditional love and support from my family, my colleagues and my friends.

The only question that remains is whether or not I will find love: that ultimate desire deeply embedded in our DNA, that amazing, indescribable combination of devotion, trust, humor, communication, respect and passion. Ah! The perfect relationship martini mix—shaken or stirred, perhaps with extra olives on the side.

I knew I would need some time to heal; my heart felt bruised. There was a time when I really thought Simon and I would spend the rest of our lives together. But once I realized the relationship ended, I was ready for some fun. I prayed that the universe would send me a guy with whom I could have wild monkey sex. It only took a few weeks of manifestation, and life sent me Jesus.

Chapter Two

JESUS
Jesus Picked Me Up in a Bar
(Or Did I Pick Him?)

July 2004

TO GET OVER my breakup, I had been hoping to meet a guy just for great sex with no emotional strings. A few weeks after my trip to Hawaii, I went to one of my local happy hour spots, and there was Jesus. We were sitting next to one another at the bar, and we started chatting. He was cute enough, though not my usual type, wearing a light blue Lacoste shirt, Levi jeans and leather flip-flops. He was very engaging. Before I knew it, we were making out in my car. My wish had come true. But as we all learn at some point, we must be careful what we wish for.

For the next few months, we hung out, talked and laughed a lot, but mostly we had sex. He was very randy, the classic Latin lover, and after two years in a mostly sexless relationship, I was ready for that situation. We often met for happy hour. Soon enough we would end up in the parking lot, on a lounge chair by the Ritz-Carlton pool at 2 a.m. (I hope they don't have security cameras!), or in the women's bathroom. On the occasions we made it back to his apartment, he would say, "Drop your pants" and go down on me right there on the living room sofa. Wherever. Whenever. Who was I to refuse? Would you?

It may sound shallow, but at that point in time, neither of us wanted a "relationship." We got from each other what we needed: sex. When I don't want to get emotionally involved with a man, I have a rule to keep him out of my bedroom, so Jesus never spent the night. I'd go to his house or we'd make out on my couch, but he never came upstairs. This arrangement worked for both of us, and no one was complaining.

Although Jesus was great for a fun night out—or in—he certainly had his flaws (but don't we all?). He had terrible gas, his bathroom was filthy, and he was a backseat driver.

Growing up in LA, I know how to parallel park, and most of the time the parking at his cramped apartment complex was really tight. No matter how deftly I negotiated a space, as I was turning the steering wheel he would always say in his thick Texan accent, "Crank it!" Safely in the spot, he would say, "Great job." I would shoot him a look. It was incredibly annoying. Once in his apartment, he would say, "Drop your pants." All would be forgiven until the next time.

Even though this relationship was just for sex, I found it hard to ignore the state of his bathroom: Disgusting with a capital "D." I have never seen such a moldy shower curtain. I teased him about it, hoping he would clean it for my sake, but it stayed nasty, hanging there growing more mold. For all I know he still has the same one. Ah, the bachelor life!

Sadly, I can't tell you how many times we performed our little routine. He'd say, "Crank it," we'd walk in the house, he'd say, "Drop your pants," I'd sit on the couch, he'd go down on me, I'd zip my pants, I'd leave. I must admit, even his friends were a little taken aback by my behavior. There was a strange aura of respect and confusion whenever we all spent time together.

In the mornings, as he got up to walk to that bathroom, he would fart away, jolting me awake with the jarring noise and smell. After a few rude, smelly mornings, I asked him, "Are you cranking it?" We both laughed, but it wasn't long before I stopped staying over to avoid the fart-fest. Jesus and the circumstances of our relationship were all very male and rather obnoxious, but the sex—especially the head—was great.

Jesus definitely was filling the sexual void that existed in my relationship with Simon, but he wasn't a guy that I could have a "real" relationship with. More frequently, little things started to bug me, like the old baseball hat he always wore, and the over-the-top creepy feeling I got from having sex on his foldout couch mere hours after his visiting parents had slept on it. I could still smell them on the blankets.

After a while, we just drifted apart. Phone calls (read: booty calls) stopped being returned, dates started to be broken; he became unavailable to me and I was happy to move on. We remain friends, occasionally text messaging and emailing each other. I still see him around every once in a while at our mutual happy hour spots. Every time I bump into him, I remember that I do want more—something closer to the "whole package."

Chapter Three

The Science Project Seeds Are Planted

July 2004

Today, the seed plants are some of the most important organisms on earth. Life on land as we know it is shaped largely by the activities of seed plants.

—University of California—Berkley, Museum of Paleontology

SEEDS ARE THE beginning of life, a tiny mass of cells containing the genetic material to form new beings. From ancient to modern life, from a morning cup of Joe to a basic cotton t-shirt, all things organic start as seeds. Similar to the reproductive biology of flowers, humans too are the end result of a seeding process. We both have male and female parts needed for proliferation. However, the idea of male sperm and female eggs needing wind or insects for fertilization may not go over well, at least not in the crowds in which I socialize.

Jesus blew into my life, not unlike the wind, just a month after the breakup with Simon. I must have manifested fertile soil, because I asked the universe for casual, no-strings sex, and I got it. Was I playing into a genetic impulse? According to the August 15, 1994, *Time* magazine cover story, "Infidelity: It May Be in Our Genes," everything comes back to the survival of genetic codes.

Jesus was my flash point where the sparks, seeds and rumblings of my year-long social science project began to take root. This got me thinking: Did the lack of sex and physical intimacy with Simon trigger some prevailing, basic animal behavior in me? Hmm...more research was needed.

In the Human Genome Project, from a February 2001 publication, the data suggests that we have around 30,000 genes. It's crazy, but true: Humans are just barely bigger genome-wise than a corn plant. Jesus, metaphorically speaking, had become my seed.

Chapter Four

Room #104 and Neighbor Peter

When a Man Buys You Drinks, Is He Entitled to More?

August–September 2004

FEELING I HAD sown my wild oats with Jesus, meeting men took a backseat to rest of my life. I was disenchanted with the male of the species and still processing the split with Simon; I needed a break. I threw myself into my work, also making an effort to be even more present in my yoga practice and volunteer commitments.

At the time, I was volunteering with an organization that provides grief counseling for teenagers who have lost their parents. It was very heavy stuff. Coupled with a two-hour bumper-to-bumper commute to the Valley on the 405 Freeway, I was exhausted. I have worked over twenty years with homeless and runaway youth in shelters, squats and out on the streets. Working with youth who have lost parents was equally difficult, but ultimately rewarding. It really helped put things in perspective. All my problems aside, I am blessed with an amazing life.

Twice a month, the grief counselors got together for "supervision" to talk about our clients, what was happening with us personally and in our group sessions. As counselors, that time was extremely beneficial and reassuring. On my way home one night after supervision, I went to the Baja Cantina, a Mexican restaurant and a local hangout spot, a true fixture in the neighborhood. At times, it is a major meat market. It was a Tuesday evening in September, so I figured it would be quiet and mellow. I was in no mood for the pick-up scene, but I left it to fate: If there was a parking spot out front, I would take it as a sign.

My plan was to have dinner, one drink, and go straight home. It was the end of a long day, and I was feeling somewhat drained from supervision. As I drove up Washington Boulevard, there was a spot right in front. I guess fate intervened. With the new issue of *Rolling Stone* magazine in hand, I took a seat on one of the two open stools at the bar and ordered a Caesar salad and an 1800 Cuervo tequila neat—the bartender knew me and made it a double. My only intention was to read the magazine and call it an early night. The very last thing on my mind was meeting men. Famous last words!

Sitting there with my salad, tequila and *Rolling Stone*, a guy around thirty years old with a red crew cut started talking to me. Athletic and toned with big brown eyes, he was very attractive, dressed in baggy jeans and a t-shirt with a large company logo across the chest. I had never heard of the company on his shirt, so I asked him about it.

He was a professional paintball player; the logo on the shirt was for one of his sponsors. I had no idea people made a living playing paintball! Actually, I thought that trend went out in the nineties. Mr. Paintball was in LA on business from Philadelphia, taking meetings for a video game he was creating. Interesting! We exchanged names, but for the life of me, I can't remember his.

We were having an engaging conversation; I was getting quite an education about the world of paintball. After about thirty minutes, a man sat on the other side of me. Everyone at the bar was elbow to elbow. The new man to my right introduced himself as Peter. He was a tall, heavy-set, olive skinned, "rico suave" kind of guy, dressed in a hip-hop style with some serious bling going on. His head was shaved clean, and he looked a little closer to my age.

Although I was clearly wrapped up in conversation with another man, Peter started talking to me. I became very aware that I was sitting between two guys, although I was not out to meet men. They were both talking to me, but frankly, it didn't seem like a pick-up. I was still working on my salad and drink, but I'd given up on the magazine. Peter offered to buy me another tequila. At first I refused, but he was exceedingly insistent, so I accepted; it all seemed pretty innocent.

He told me he was a PR person for a hip-hop record label, and it became clear he was not just being nice. Every time I ordered another drink, he was adamant about paying for it, making sure the bartender took his money instead of mine. I thought, *Hmmm, he's very aggressive, but he seems nice enough.* It turned out he lived just around the corner from me. It's always nice to have new friends that are within walking distance, but really, what was going on? I was just minding my own business, and there I was with these two guys. It was getting late, and I wanted to wake up early the next morning for yoga.

The three of us chatted for a while, and then Mr. Paintball said, "Hey, why don't you come back to my room? I'm staying right next door." I said, "Yeah, sure. I'll go back to your room." His confidence and candor were a major turn on, not to mention his success in the world of paintball. I'm always attracted to men who excel at things they are passionate about. Actually, I think that is attractive in anyone—male or female.

I felt bad about leaving Neighbor Peter, who had bought all my drinks, but I felt more like I was accepting them to avoid an argument. Plus Mr. Paintball was very appealing. I thanked Peter for the drinks, gave him my cell phone number and email address, and told him to call me sometime. He promised he would.

It was a very short walk to Mr. Paintball's hotel. I was not really sure what to expect, and truthfully, I was not thinking of sex. Call me naïve, but I did not think he was interested in that either. It just seemed like we were having good conversation, enjoying each other's company. We took the elevator up to his floor, entered room #104, and he kissed me without missing a beat. I thought*, Well, that's not what I expected. Maybe I should go*. It was not "magic," but it was good. He was raring to go. His body was impressive: washboard stomach, hairless smooth skin, and he smelled good. I was sure I had sprouted little devil horns and a tail—so much for going straight home.

He lifted me up, and making his intentions very clear, put me on the bed. I was lying on the hotel bedspread, when I thought, *Oh god, they never wash these things.* I imagined the stomach-turning stains and bodily fluids that might be hiding in the multi-colored polyester. I lay there in my favorite white, designer skirt with a hot guy hovering over me, his tongue in my mouth, worrying about the spilled pizza sauce (and worse) of past occupants. I would most likely never see this man again. Was he worth ruining my favorite skirt?

Suddenly, his hand was touching the inside of my upper thigh, and I forgot all about the stain and germ-ridden bedspread. He was a skilled lover. Perhaps it was just because we knew we would never see one another again, or because he'd watched a lot of porn (within minutes, he made some specific requests that indicated the latter), but the sex was raw and uninhibited. After several hours, we fell asleep; it was around 3:00 a.m. when I awoke. *Should I stay, or should I go?*

He was sound asleep as I snuck out of the room. Safely home, I brushed my teeth, washed my face and got into my bed, glad be there alone.

Feeling the effects of my night of debauchery, I got up around 9:00 a.m.; I'd already missed yoga. There were three calls from Peter on my cell phone—two from the night before and one first thing in the morning. I also found numerous emails in my inbox.

It freaked me out that he was being so aggressive, a borderline stalker. I ignored him and set off for the gym to sweat out Room #104 and the 1800. I wracked my brain to remember Room #104's name. My horns and tail were surely visible. I had offered to take him to the airport the next day, so I went back to the hotel to find him.

Usually cool and calm in most situations, my heart was pounding as I rode up in the elevator and knocked on the door. He opened it and invited me in. It was awkward; we were both uneasy, but we survived. As we were talking, he told me about his girlfriend back home—the girlfriend that he lived with. I asked him if he had these out-of-town flings all the time. He looked me straight in the eye and said, "No, this is the first time I have ever done anything like this." I can still see his face at that moment. I'm still sure he was lying. Room #104 was not only a professional paintball player, he was a professional "player," and I took part in his game. But I had been up for the adventure, whatever the outcome.

I was still not able to remember his name when we said goodbye, but I didn't care any more. He was a liar, and not someone I would want in my world. I only saw him one more time, in the pages of a paintball magazine about a month later. I was at a Barnes & Noble bookstore, looking at dating books for research. I saw the one and only paintball magazine in the periodicals section and thumbing through the pages, I found Room #104! Well, I'm pretty sure it was him. The man in the photo wore a helmet with a face guard, but a bit of his red hair was visible, and I'd recognize that body anywhere. At least I knew he didn't lie about his profession. Along with the dating books and an Italian *Vogue,* I bought the paintball magazine, smiling as the clerk gave me a quizzical look. I keep it with all my other research for the book; it's my souvenir of the day I became a social scientist.

The day I said goodbye to Room #104, I returned home to find my email inbox and cell phone filled with messages from Neighbor Peter. I was unsure if it was best to call him or ignore him. He was obviously eager, but he did seem like a nice guy. He just lacked girl-skills. I called him back and agreed to go on a date with him that weekend. Thinking back, I tried to get out of our initial date, but he was once again very persistent. I gave him brownie points for his willingness to fight to have a date with me.

We went to Mr. Chow, one of my favorite restaurants in Los Angeles. He seemed like a decent-hearted man. Under his gruff exterior is a man looking for companionship—aren't we all? Although he wore way too much cologne and was a little rough around the edges, we had a few things in common. We talked about his job at the record label and my own connections within the music industry.

Things were going fine until he asked me to feed him. *What? Is he kidding?* I thought. He wanted me to feed him pieces of the green shrimp, just like a romantic couple in a movie. It was a very awkward moment—definitely not romantic. I really just wanted the date to be over, but he'd been so generous, I felt it would be rude to cut things short.

After dinner, he talked me into a nightcap at the Ritz-Carlton. We sat on one of the big couches in the bar area, where I sipped hot tea and he had a mixed drink. As we sat there talking, he slid his hand across my hip and commented, "You're not wearing underwear." I nodded confirmation of his suspicion. I was wearing a very tight dress, and I consider panty lines to be a big fashion don't. Even the Hollywood standard, Cosabella, would be visible. If the general public knew just how many women "go commando," no one would be shocked by my confession.

In a split second, his hand was up my tight, black, Dolce and Gabbana dress right there on the Ritz-Carlton couch. He leaned in and whispered in my ear all the things he wanted to do. I must admit I got a tingle in my nether region; I was still pretty charged from Room #104, although our encounter had been three nights earlier. The next thing I knew, Neighbor Peter and I were in the pool area on a lounge chair. I had a little Jesus déjà vu moment, and then he pulled out his "thing." It was shockingly large; without even thinking I told him, "Put that THING away." I was out of there—date officially over!

When I got home that night, I started to sneeze uncontrollably. His cologne was stuck on my skin, in my hair and in my clothing. I showered before I went to bed, putting my cologne-drenched dress into a Ziploc bag to seal off his stench. First thing in the morning, I drove to the dry cleaner and handed the bag of toxic material to Jill for a complete decontamination.

Someplace inside Neighbor Peter is the decent-hearted man I saw that the first time we met, but I was never able to pull back enough layers to find it. He did a great job of putting on a macho, womanizing act to keep me from seeing his true core. The Sunday after our date, he called first thing in the morning, interrupting my weekly ritual of doing the bills, practicing yoga and getting ready for the new week.

"Hi Jennifer, it's Peter. Why don't you come over and sit on my face?"

I wanted to heave. "No. I don't think so," was my disgusted reply.

"Well, do you want to go to Manhattan Beach this afternoon? There's a food festival. It should be really cool."

"No. I have yoga."

"How about we meet later for dinner, then?"

"No. I like to take a sauna after yoga class and have a relaxing night alone." Sunday is my day, and I was not about to change my routine for him.

The next day, I received five voicemails, along with several emails from Peter. This was abnormal behavior. I let him know that his actions made me uncomfortable and I didn't want to see him again. That has yet to stop him from contacting me.

One evening a few weeks later, I met a friend for dinner in Hollywood. It just so happened that Peter's company was having an event at a nearby club. He called to invite me, but I declined.

"Well, do you think you could give me a ride home?" he asked.

He went on to explain that he didn't have his car since his company had picked him up in a limo. It didn't seem like a big deal. The club was ten minutes from the restaurant. Since we live just a few blocks from one another, it all seemed harmless, so I agreed. I picked him up from the party and about halfway home, he realized he'd left his keys at the club.

"What do you want to do?" I asked.

"I'll call and have one of the workers from my office drive the van over and bring my keys. I know exactly where they are."

Exasperated, I pulled into the gas station under a lamppost. I was exhausted and just wanted to be home—not to mention I was in no mood to be with him. We were there for only a couple of minutes when a police car pulled in. Since I'd had a few glasses of wine at dinner, I moved the car to another section of the gas station lot. I didn't want our loitering to draw any undue attention.

He got freaked out and shouted, "Why did you do that?"

"Well I had wine with dinner, and the police are parked right there. I think it looks weird that we're just sitting here in the car. It's LA, Peter. Bizarre occurrences and violent crimes happen here all the time. We look conspicuous."

We had a huge argument, which was par for the course. From day one it seemed that most everything with him was an argument, from buying me drinks to going on a date with him. I'm not an argumentative person, and I found it very manipulative of him. I was spending time with this man I didn't even like, just to avoid an argument.

He continues to call and email me a few times a month. I do not return his calls, and I only send him very short email replies. I will respond once for every five or six emails I receive. A typical exchange goes something like this:

From: Peters_email@**.com**
Hi…
Peter

From: Peters_email@**.com**
Hey,
How's it going?

From: Peters_email@**.com**
Just working…and you?
Moved to Venice.
Peter

From: Peters_email@**.com**
Wanna meet for a drink at Za Zen?
Peter

From: Jennifer@**.com**
I will be out of town till May 1.

From: Peters_email@**.com**
Where u going?
-P

From: Peters_email@**.com**
Guess not, huh.
-P

His persistence makes me uncomfortable, but no matter how curt or distant I am, he never goes away. In a strange twist of fate, as I was writing his chapter of the book, I saw him standing in front of the gym I go to. He had told me he was a member there, but I had never seen him at the club in the past. With thumping heart and held breath, I put my head in my gym bag and walked right by unnoticed. I dodged that bullet. I hope to never see him again.

Chapter Five

The Science Project

July 2004–July 2005

The roots of science, however, ran deep, stretching back to the period before the appearance of civilization.

—Dr. Stephen F. Mason, *The History of Sciences*

science (sns) *n.*

1. a. The observation, identification, description, experimental investigation, and theoretical explanation of phenomena.
   b. Such activities restricted to a class of natural phenomena.
   c. Such activities applied to an object of inquiry or study.
2. Methodological activity, discipline, or study: *I've got packing a suitcase down to a science.*
3. An activity that appears to require study and method: *the science of purchasing.*
4. Knowledge, especially that gained through experience.

—http://www.thefredictionary.com/science

AT ITS ORIGIN, science is traceable to the earliest development of tools by men of the Stone Age, dating back to 2,000,000 BCE-3,000,000 BCE. Since then man has been driven to learn and discover. Even today, as illustrated by websites such as Science Daily, we continue to explore and ask questions about life's mysteries, from how the Didgeridoo improves sleep to examining the dust currently "swirling around a young star" that NASA's Spitzer Space Telescope discovered. It just so happens that the dust contains the same gaseous precursors to DNA and protein in a region where rocky planets such as Earth are believed to have been born. It's mind boggling to think about how far we have come in the last 200 years alone in our search of new frontiers.

Jesus, Room # 104 and Neighbor Peter planted the first seeds of my own investigation. As of September 12, 2004, my dating life was in the germination stage of becoming a study on human nature, mating and the male of the species.

I said to one of my girlfriends over dinner that my evenings with Moldy-Shower-Curtain Jesus, Mr.-Paintball-Cheats-on-His-Girlfriend Room #104, and Cologne Ree-king-Stalker Neighbor Peter had given me pause. "I feel like I'm conducting a science project."

It was as if an eighteen-wheel semi truck had run over me and I survived to tell the story. Dating and mating rituals are compelling and incredibly riveting acts of human behavior. In just a matter of days, I'd gone from being in my own world of grief counseling, work and yoga to X-rated debauchery with Room #104 and utter revulsion with Neighbor Peter. Jesus had started it all just two months before.

With the seeds planted, I began to mull over Newton's Third Law of Motion: For every action there is an equal and opposite reaction. Just like a plant needs certain environmental factors for growth, humans cannot touch one another without being touched back. With the hamster and wheel busily spinning in my mind, I realized that I was onto something.

I have always been intensely interested in human behavior. I've read many books on the subject; I have traveled all over the world and seen humanity at its extreme best and worst. In my personal experience, there doesn't seem to be any really honest information for women, or men, about dating, mating, attraction and love. According to the World Health Organization, sexual intercourse occurs more than a hundred million times daily worldwide. Based on those numbers, you would think that there would be more honest books on the subject. There are few works that address making good decisions or share real-life stories—the kind you would never tell at the family Thanksgiving table. These stories can touch a place deep within you and resonate.

I feel that one of the keys to life is to operate from a place of true compassion and honesty. I believe very strongly that by being honest we all have the capability to open up new and important dialogues. In an effort to start these conversations, I decided to make my dating life an experiment. When testing any theory, you sometimes get unexpected results. In the name of science, I acknowledged the importance of looking limitlessly for answers, even if they contradicted my preconceived ideas.

That evening I headed to the local bookstore to see what was being written about the baffling world of dating and human nature in general. With this goal, and the understanding that "science does not and can not produce absolute and unquestionable truth,"[2] I began my mission. Let the science project begin.

Chapter Six

Dating Books Debunked

Let's face it: a date is a job interview that lasts all night. The only difference between a date and a job interview is that in not many job interviews is there a chance you'll end up naked at the end of it.

—Jerry Seinfeld

THERE ARE MANY places to get relationship and dating advice. Our modern-day airwaves are chock full of opinions, as are our families and friends. It can be difficult to figure out who to trust. My grandmother and I always had a very tight bond. She was a strong woman: an artist with dedicated family values, she was considered to be somewhat of a bohemian in her day. In my opinion, she was a truly amazing woman. When I was young, I marveled at my grandparents' marriage. I remember asking her how she managed to stay devoted to my grandfather and keep their love alive. She said, "I have always kept some mystery in the marriage."

What a wonderful nugget of advice. She was not saying to play games, but to keep a place within yourself that is sacred. At her age, I'm certain that she did not read that in *Glamour* or *Cosmopolitan* but learned it from her own life experience. While I do agree that a certain amount of mystery is important to a relationship, at the end of the day, the key is being honest on all levels.

My parents also gave me some words of wisdom about what it takes to sustain a loving relationship: both people must have willingness to work at it, be open, have honest communication with a touch of humor and the ability to compromise. They were high school sweethearts and have been very happily married for almost fifty years—they're still very much in love. They must be doing something right. My maternal grandmother shared with my parents that "each person needs to give one hundred percent to the relationship." She and my grandfather were also married over fifty years.

I come from a long line of lasting, happy relationships, and because of the examples around me, I have learned that while no relationship is perfect, the ideal is possible. There is no reason to settle. As long as you have honesty, communication, humor and the ability to be flexible, a solid relationship is one hundred percent attainable.

But if it's really that simple, why do we need the countless movies, TV shows, magazine articles, websites and books to guide us? Next time you are at a newsstand, notice the number of cover stories about finding, attracting and keeping a mate. I read many books researching this phenomenon. What I read astonished me: so many rules to follow, as many ways to "find love" as there are possibilities in life. That is valid. Everyone is different. What works for one person may not work for the next. So who should you believe? Mom, Dad, Grandma, Grandpa, *Cosmo, Men's Health*, Dr. Phil, Oprah? There is an exhaustive laundry list of advice constantly being waved in our faces.

A good way to get beyond the advice gurus: Begin with a healthy belief in yourself. It's important to always follow your heart and your gut. It's much more important to do what feels right than to do what the media or other people tell you to do. Throughout the course of my own life's discovery process, I have mopped up myriad tears with countless rolls of Green Forest toilet paper while seeking to find my own answers; I have also laughed at myself and enjoyed the journey. We all have the answers inside ourselves, but sometimes it's hard to sift through the static to find them.

For me the journey has made me the person I am. I embrace it as a positive. What I realize is that it's more about the journey than the end result. In life, and in relationships, we are constantly learning, changing and evolving. Every end is a new beginning, and when the door hits your butt on the way out, a new door will open.

Most of the dating books on today's market are more concerned with how you behave than what kind of person you are. Why base a relationship on behavior that is not your own? Why pretend to be someone you're not? How long will you be able to keep up a charade like that? What will happen when you finally start being yourself?

These are the questions the dating books do not answer. As I combed through countless pages of advice, it became even more evident that the answer is to not play by someone else's "rules," but to truthfully follow your own heart and do what feels right for you. That is my advice. Debunking some of the more outrageous myths about "what men want" or "how to be a great date" is an ideal place to start.

In *How to Make a Man Fall in Love with You*, Tracy Cabot, PhD outlines what she calls "The Love Plan." It is an approach that she swears by; her method is to attract and keep love. The cover of the book even claims it is "The Fail Proof, Fool Proof Method!" How do you fool proof love? She goes on to say that it has worked for her and "everyone else who has tried it." But no one can force love or attraction.

I read on, though I was bothered that Dr. Cabot would suggest "a plan," a map for love. While Dr. Cabot did make some good points, much of her plan consists of manipulation and pretense—trying to elicit certain reactions by using what she calls "spells" and positive reinforcement. That feels like game playing to me. I closed the book when I came to the section called "Why Indifference Works." More games. Life is complex. It cannot be broken down to a simple game of checkers. Love and life do not fit into little squares.

Dr. Cabot's book is in complete contrast to one I found that offered practical, common-sense advice for women—*The Real Rules: How to Find the Right Man for the Real You,* by Barbara De Angelis, PhD. Real Rule 4 is, "Don't play games." She goes on to say, "The dictionary defines the word game as a form of play, or sport, a scheme, plan or trick...When love becomes a game, everybody loses." No one wants to be tricked into love.

Date Like a Man by Myreah Moore and Jodie Gould contained some good information. I appreciated the fact that it went straight to the point, especially in the chapter "How to Have Sex Like a Man: Sex Tips from Men That You Can't Live/Date Without." This chapter goes from the difference between love and lust to frank advice about deep-throating and masturbation. But it is still very rules-based: more planning what to say and when to say it. That feels controlling and unnatural. It doesn't leave enough room to be yourself.

Finally, I turned to the granddaddy of them all. I spent about twenty minutes skimming through *The Rules* by Ellen Fein and Sherrie Schneider before I became completely overwhelmed. Laying it aside, I remembered that a guy I was dating had called and left a message. I decided to call him back, breaking Rule 5: "Don't Call Him and Rarely Return His Calls." According to the book, if I am "following *The Rules* religiously, there is no reason to call him." Being the feisty sort of gal I am, I decided to take my chances and take a walk on the wild side.

I could almost hear the Helen Reddy song "I Am Woman" playing in the background. As I dialed his number there was no heart racing, no butterflies in my stomach. After a few rings, he answered, sounding happy to hear my voice. I mentioned that I was breaking "Rule 5" and asked him what he thought about that. "It's absurd. If you never call a guy back he will think you aren't interested and not call you." Fascinating. That's what I was thinking too, especially in this age of strong female role models.

After hanging up, I realized what I really needed was the Man-O-Pinion. While I have clear ideas, I needed to go straight to the source. I enlisted a total of sixteen men: eight of my male friends, some men I have dated, and a few strangers to get a wide array of opinions.

As with all of my studies, the sample included men of varying ages, races, religions, economic and relationship statuses. From a variety of dating books, I assembled these "rules" women are told to follow. I presented each man with ten survey questions, derived from several dating book scenarios, and asked for their honest opinions.

I shared a sample of recommended dating behavior from the book *Date Like a Man,* which prompted my first questions.

> **Step #1:** Date Him. Do you like the guy? Do you think that you have a lot in common? Go out with him two or three times to see if you click. Let him woo you.
>
> **Step #2:** Disappear. Make yourself totally unavailable. He'll call you and get your answering machine. If he drops by your house, the blinds will be drawn. Keep him in a state of deprivation for about a week.
>
> **Step #3:** Reestablish Contact. After a week's hiatus pick up the phone and pop back into his life. Don't apologize for your absence or make excuses. Just tell him you've been very busy. Then ask him, "What is new with you?"

This reminded me of the age-old question: Who calls who and when? In my thinking, a whole week is wrong; any mate-worthy guy would think it was weird and scary, almost mean. If you went out with someone a few times, had a really good time, then he suddenly disappeared, how would you feel? If a man did that to me, I would not want to see him again. A man who is attracted by this kind of manipulative behavior is not a "keeper." The authors of *Date Like a Man* say they "learned these steps from men," but who are these men? The men I surveyed had other ideas.

Of the test group, 63% feel there should be "no rules on how many days to wait" and agree that the burden of calling rests equally with both the man and the woman. Although, as Man #1 responded, "It's nice to have a girl make the move once in a while." A whopping 86% of the men surveyed expressed dislike of "playing games or sending and receiving false messages, like the whole disappearance thing."

"Either you are interested or not, simple," Man #13 stated. But there were a few diehard traditionalists in the group: "The man must be the one to make the call two to three days later. If you really like the girl, four days is the best."

So much attention has already been given to *The Rules*, it's an easy target. It's been examined, quoted, praised, reviled and spoofed at every turn—and there's a good reason. A set of rules, in my opinion, sets you up for disaster. Once again, I turned to the men to debunk these "truths" Mrs. Fein and Mrs. Schneider hold to be self-evident.

Rule 3 forbids "staring at men." I asked the men if they liked women to make eye contact with them in social situations. The response was overwhelmingly positive—100% of the men loved the idea. "Confidence is a wonderful thing," said Man #4, and Man #12 added, "Eye contact creates connection." So much for the shrinking violet routine!

But while phone-calling and eye-flirting are welcomed by most men, the group was split on controversial Rule 4, which tells women not to pay or meet a man halfway on a date. Claiming that "men love a challenge," the authors of *The Rules* state that the worst thing we can do is make it easy for them. Man #2 encapsulated their theory: "Allowing me to pay makes me feel good—kind of a macho, 'taking care of the lady' thing—but if she offers to go 'Dutch,' it's a nice way for her to let me know to cool my jets."

Of the men surveyed, 38% appreciate the offer when it's made, but would insist on paying. Man #4 responded, "It's a nice gesture if she offers to pay, and always appreciated, but that won't happen. Chivalry isn't completely dead." But 43% like women to share the financial aspects of dating. "We are initially doing the dating thing to acquaint. I am not doing you a favor or vice versa. I do not want to meet a woman espousing traditional values. The 'he always pays' value is anachronistic and smacks of inequality," Man #13 reasons. Man # 6 agrees that if a woman offers to pay, "it shows she is thoughtful, independent, and doesn't buy into traditional rules."

Going back to phone etiquette, I asked the group of men what they thought of Rule 5: "Don't Call Him and Rarely Return His Call." The authors add, "There is no reason to call," and that "he should be calling you." The responses are in keeping with their assessment of the *Date Like a Man* "steps." A sizeable 80% agrees that if a woman never calls, a man assumes she's not interested and will move on. "Men are as insecure as women," Man #13 reminds us, "and [we] need reassurance. There is no harm in letting a man know you care for him, and a call goes a long way in that direction." Men also feel, again, that the dating rituals should be shared: Man #16 noted, "I like it when a woman calls me just as much as

I call her. It shows respect for each other." Respect is essential to any relationship. Wouldn't you like to know from the get-go that you are both operating on the same wavelength or playing on the same team?

But how much contact is too much? The strategy of Rule 13 is, "Don't See Him More than Once or Twice a Week." The men are split on this one, the answers ranging from two to three times a week (still above *The Rules*' maximum) to "If I really liked her, every day!" Two dates a week was the panel's minimum recommendation, and 70% suggested a two to three date maximum in the early stages, building to three to five dates a week if things progress. But in all cases, the women are welcome to call to make the plans!

Now let's get down to the real burning questions. How far should you go physically on the first date? Rule 15 warns that "No More than Casual Kissing on the First Date" is acceptable. I also wanted to know if "going further" has been a deal breaker or changed the man's opinion of the woman he is courting. I was surprised at how many men agreed with Rule 15.

Only 30% express a "go with what feels right" kind of attitude. A majority of the men surveyed are a bit more traditional when it comes to sex early on in a relationship. "There is something cool about not going all the way on a first date," Man #8 said, "and maybe taking it slow." Man #13 concurs: "Getting physical too soon just takes some of the early anticipation away. That is crucial and propels the relationship." But of all of the respondents, only 10% reported that moving too quickly or too slowly would change their opinion of the woman they were dating. Most agreed with Man #1's assessment: "Sometimes two people click right away, and things move along rapidly. Sometimes things take a while."

So overall, I'd say the men I interviewed didn't think much of playing by a set of rules. The overwhelming consensus seemed to be what I have felt all along: Do what feels right to you. Of course, I had a few questions myself, based on my own experiences. In regards to online dating and other common life situations, I wanted to know if men liked women to contact them. While 50% had not participated in online dating, those who did were 99% in favor of women asking them for a date. Man #7 said it all: "I wouldn't be on there if I did not want to be approached."

What about being approached at a bar or another social setting? Men absolutely want women to introduce themselves. "I like a woman with enough confidence to walk up and chat," Man #4 responded. Although, fellow women, Man #14 wants you to watch the booze: "As long as it's done with a professional approach, not from a drunken sleazy approach. That's a big turn-off to gentlemen." But as Man #15 so eloquently put it, "Hells yeah!" was by far the most popular reaction.

Back to sex: I heard the men talk about playing it cool and waiting for the "right time" to get physical with a woman, but what I really wanted to know was how many dates they were willing to hang around without it. For the most part, they stuck to their guns. Man #2 is willing to wait "until I feel like the chick is not interested in ever having sex with me," while Man #5 says, "as many as it takes before it feels right." The men who put a number on it range their answers from three to five to ten dates- so, there really does seem to be a no-set-rule, play-it-by-ear thing here. Do what your gut tells you to do, and whatever happens, you will be able to deal with the outcome.

When things do get serious, talk of marriage can be a delicate subject. I wondered how men felt about living together before marriage. 80% feel it's a good idea and "would encourage it." Of the married and divorced men in the survey, only one thought it was a bad idea. Man #16 shared that "at my wedding, during my speech I said, 'I bought the cow.' We were together for five years and lived together for one year before we got married." So it can happen. Perhaps Aunt Ruth was wrong in her Thanksgiving dinner living together lecture!

Additional input:
Things Men Thought You Should Know

Man #9—Guys like to be flattered but challenged.

Man #7—Dating is not a game. Relationships are not a game.

Man #4—I find hard rules to be confining. Better to adjust to whatever circumstances arise.

Though my sample group ranged broadly in age, relationship status, religion, race and economic level, they share a common ground straight across the board: confident women. Although they enjoy being approached, called on the phone or asked for dates, it is also clear that men still like to be men in a more traditional sense. So while you can be confident, self-sufficient and able to hold your own, you can still let him open the car door or pull out the chair. For the record, maybe it's best to listen to Your-Own-O-Pinion when interacting with the male of the species. Based on the Man-O-Pinion, it looks as though they agree.

Most dating books focus on women trying to attract men. Something about that seems unbalanced. Why does a woman need a manual, yet a man just has to be himself? Well, it turns out there are books for men. My friend Mike suggested that I read *How to Drive Your Woman Wild in Bed* by Graham Masterton and *How to Succeed with Women* by Ron Louis and David Copeland.

I was not surprised to find that the content was less about changing one's own behavior and more focused on common sense suggestions about treating yourself and others with respect. There were "do this, do that" sections, but not on par with the books geared toward women. I liked the parts where they talk about good hygiene, keeping your car clean and wearing clean clothing—which are less about "rules for dating" and more about showing respect for yourself and others.

Not long ago, I ran into an old friend at the local nail salon. There he was, looking handsome as two women gave him a manicure and pedicure. I told him I was glad to see him in the chair. "Bad hands and feet can be a big turnoff for me." He laughed and added, "I learned a long time ago that a small amount of hygiene goes a long way with women."

To gain insight into how men perceive these books, I took them out in public to read. I found that men wanted to check them out; the interest was there, but reading such a book seems unmanly or girly. One of my male friends said that every man should read *How to Drive Your Woman Wild.* "Women are confusing and it would be nice to have a manual," he quipped. But perhaps the stigma of self-help still makes it taboo.

In my studies, I did come across a few books that spoke to me in my own language: *The Real Rules: How to Find the Right Man for the Real You* by Barbara De Angelis, PhD; *If the Buddha Dated*, by Charlotte Kasl, PhD; and *Care of the Soul*, by Thomas Moore, which is less about relationships and more about life.

These books offer some very solid advice, but they go

beyond that by offering natural and common sense approaches to interaction and attraction.

Dr. De Angelis discourages all the game playing that goes on between men and women. "Real Rule 14: Be Honest about Your Feelings" caught my attention with its good, solid insights. "Communication that works always has honesty as its foundation. It's when you are dishonest about how you feel in relationships that things get messy, unpleasant, and complicated." She does go on to say that this honesty needs to be integrated with common sense.

Human behavior may be confusing, as we each have unique lives that give us our own special brand of individuality—and that is a beautiful thing! However, there is one thing, I believe, that will lead you in the right direction. A certain amount of self-understanding is important to create healthy relationships. The first step is to look inward; the second is to look outward. Of course, all of this self-awareness can be difficult.

In *Care of the Soul*, Thomas Moore writes, "We sometimes talk about love lightly, not acknowledging how powerful and lasting it can be. We always expect love to be healing and whole, and then are astonished to find that it can create hollow gaps and empty failures."

The bottom line is that love begins not just with a connection to another person, but with being true to yourself. It can't be said enough: Self-awareness and honesty not only open up your own life channels but provide you with better opportunities to receive what you give. I am talking karma here, and that sets you on the right path. When you know who you are and what you are made of, you will not be as likely to settle for less.

> A commitment to another person is always a commitment to know ourselves and do whatever it takes to fulfill our agreements. If we promise to be truthful, we commit to a deep level of inner awareness and to confronting any fear that blocks us from being truthful.
>
> —*If the Buddha Dated* by Charlotte Kasl, PhD

While writing the closing thoughts for this chapter, my friend RJ Joseph, a Cree Indian I met in Sedona, Arizona shared a powerful story with me. In an email, he wrote, "An old Indian woman once told me, 'The longest journey you'll ever make in life is the journey from your head to your heart.' She then drew a line with her finger from my forehead, down my nose and chin, to my heart." RJ concluded, "I just remembered this the other day, and thought I would share it with you. (She was right.)"

Chapter Seven

JOHN
Rodeo vs. Ro-day-o

October 2004

DOES GEOGRAPHY REALLY matter? Does it reflect education, economics and a social status? Maybe yes, maybe no, but John and I were definitely from two different worlds. We met on Match.com.

In his photo, he was nice looking. A couple years younger than me—a non-issue in my mind—he had blue eyes; short, buzzed, blonde hair; and a soul patch, that little square of hair under the lower lip. As attractive as it is, it almost makes me wonder if he just missed a spot shaving. He was nicely groomed and very attractive. His profile was also intriguing. We shared a love of music, snowboarding and countless other outdoor sports. Oceans and mountains were our most common denominator.

I was feeling good about my decision to contact him, but when I mentioned to some of my friends that he was from an area that is not the nicest in Southern California, they were less than impressed. But I'm no snob...or am I? Trying to keep an open mind, I decided to give him a chance.

On our first date, we met at a local Mexican place close to my home in Venice. It's a comfortable but popular restaurant, low-key and unpretentious—perfect for meeting someone new. And if the date didn't go well, they make a great Caesar salad, so I knew I would be well fed. John entered late; so late, in fact, that I ordered without him, not sure that he would arrive at all.

Just before my salad came, he entered the bar area, appearing a little disoriented as he scanned the room for me. He was a dead ringer for his picture, a rarity in online dating. *Okay, so he* is *cute*, I thought. I liked his style. He was dressed in a surfer-skater-retro-rockabilly manner; he was in good shape from surfing and skating, and had a couple visible tattoos (very appealing). We made eye contact, but nothing registered in his eyes. Behind his glasses, he looked kind of glazed over, maybe even a little dull.

He clearly didn't recognize me from my online photos, or even my tattoos. I'd told him I had one on my forearm; I even told him what I'd be wearing. Dressed casually and comfortably in jeans, a tank top and flip-flops, I smiled to myself as I watched him trying to find me. It was hard not to wave or call out to him as he struggled to find me in the bar, but it was kind of humorous. I wanted to see how long it would take him to figure it out. He never did on his own. I should have known right then that he wasn't very bright.

Within minutes, my cell phone rang. It was John. "Are you here?" he asked, sounding confused. *What a Mr. Magoo*, I thought, *glasses and all*. I worried that he might walk into the wall or trip over a bar stool trying to find me. I told him where I was sitting and exactly what I was wearing. Finally, the glaze over his eyes cleared, and he joined me at the bar.

Being late without calling is a big pet peeve of mine. I was a little riled up by his lack of consideration. It was a first date—where were his manners?

Once the food and drinks came, things loosened up. We had some very basic stuff in common—a love of snowboarding, similar musical tastes—just like our profiles said we would. Our conversation consisted of the usual first date banter He was very kind and calm. My irritation waned as I began to enjoy myself.

After drinks, we decided to go for a walk along the beach in Santa Monica. It was a classic Southern California night. A cool breeze blew in from the ocean and the air was crisp. Although I can remember little of our banter, things seemed to be going well. I had almost forgotten that he was kind of dim...Or maybe the Cuervo 1800 tequila I had been drinking made him seem smarter.

I've racked my brain trying to remember what we talked about during dinner and our moonlight stroll. He didn't make any great impression on me on an intellectual level—or on any level for that matter. Typically, I have some kind of recollection of the conversations I have on first dates, but with John, there is nothing to report. Nada, zilch, zippo!

As we continued our walk, we came to a potentially dangerous area of Santa Monica. There were some gangster-looking guys drinking beer and smoking pot in the parking lot. I immediately began to shy away.

> "I don't think we should go down there," I said. The whole situation seemed sketchy, and having lived in the area for most of my life, I knew what could happen. Better to err on the side of caution.
>
> "It's okay," he said, putting on a tough guy air. "We're fine."
>
> "I don't need the hassle. Why invite trouble?" I asked. I was a little taken aback that he didn't take my concerns seriously.
>
> "It's cool. They're not going to do anything."
>
> "No, it's not cool. Why risk it?" I said. "They look like thugs, and I am not going down there."
>
> He laughed. I was surprised that he didn't respect my

feelings, nor was he looking out for my best interest and personal safety. I was beginning to believe he was *that* stupid, just blindly walking into trouble.

"Fine," I said. "Go if you want, but I am not going with you."

"OK. We don't have to," he stammered. We retreated to our cars in silence.

After a few moments of awkwardness, John broke the tension, animatedly describing the vintage car he was restoring. It sounded cool, and I was genuinely interested. I found it very sexy that he was doing all the restoration on his own. Maybe I've seen too many episodes *Monster Garage* or *Pimp my Ride,* but there's something about a man working on his car that's just a turn–on.

Then, I saw it: his vintage low rider. All the bad feelings about him left me, and I fell in lust right there. It was extremely shallow of me, I admit, but he was a part of the "Kustom Kar" culture and the whole vintage, retro thing attracted me. His Kar was that cool.

If he'd instead had a bright orange Pinto with a bumper sticker reading, "It's not how you pick the booger, it's where you put it," I would have left him right there in the parking lot, never looking back. There would have been no second chances. The possibility of love or even a make out session would have been out of the question.

But that Kar made John look a lot better. Even the fact that Mr. Magoo got a parking ticket from pure carelessness didn't faze me. Sure, he was somewhat clueless, but he was cute, and what a sexy Kar. I have never been attracted to a man based solely on what he drives, wears, owns, or the amount of money in his bank account, but there's a first time for everything. Sadly but truly, John became cool and much more fuckable because of his "ride."

I know a relationship has to be based on more, something internal and intangible, but I was curious to see where this would go. I was in uncharted territory and it felt like an adventure. We had enough surface stuff in common that I was willing to overlook some of his more questionable behavior. He'd have to work on the punctuality thing, for sure.

We shook hands good night and made plans to see one another again. The following week, I had tickets to hear one of my favorite LA bands, Ozomatli. The show was close to John's home, so I invited him to go. I felt I should give him second chance. He was likable; maybe he had been nervous. Sometimes you can't tell from just one date. Looking back, what I really wanted was to make out in his Kar. Shallow, I know! I only wanted to jump his bones and have a steamy make out session, not at his home or at my home, but in his Kar.

We met in Long Beach for the show; we danced and seemed to really connect. Once again, it could have been the drinks, but he became more likable as the evening progressed. Dancing close, he very aggressively picked me up and sat me down on a cocktail table. As the set ended, he was standing between my legs, facing me as we talked.

The sexual tension was thick. We couldn't get out of the emptying club fast enough; we were both feeling frisky, and I was thinking ahead to that Kar. I had a vision of us cruising around LA, his arm around me, mine around him, with lots of kissing right there on the newly upholstered bench front seat.

Once in the parking lot, he offered to drive me to my truck, and I eagerly hopped in. He turned the key in the ignition and revved the engine; I could feel its rumble. I was in love. I could see little heart shapes in my eyes. A little cupid with a bow and arrow hovered over my head. That big front seat was just waiting for us to be "together." It was the perfect place to make out—so we did. He was a great kisser. The sexual chemistry bubbled for a good hour or so, but it was getting late and I had a long drive home on the freeway.

In the week that followed, John and I exchanged emails and chatted a bit on the phone. He asked me why I always signed my emails with the word "best." Wow. *Did he just ask that?* I thought. I was shocked. Had he never heard that before? He wasn't trying to be obtuse; he just didn't understand what it meant. There was a long pause. I didn't know what to say. Maybe our differences were too much for a good relationship. Away from his Kar, his shine was once again becoming dull, but I swallowed another bit of doubt and made another date. Maybe the third time would be the charm.

A week or so from our previous date, John and I went to the House of Blues to see The Roots. He picked me up in The Kar. I was feeling sexy—ready for more Kar action—dressed in a tight dress and strappy heals. I had a Brazilian wax the day before, and since the dress was so tight, I decided to go out commando-style. With my hair still wet, I was feeling clean, freshly scrubbed and moisturized as I sat down on his inviting front seat.

Before the show, we stopped off at a Mexican restaurant for dinner. We talked more about hobbies and interests, but the whole time I was distracted by the way he spoke. Not to be brutal, but he just didn't sound very intelligent (Mr. Magoo is back!). I tried to put it out of my head, but it was hard to ignore. Again, I have no recollection of what we talked about. My mind wandered. *How long can I like a man just for his Kar?* I pondered. His voice droned on as he blathered about nothing in particular over chips, guacamole and drinks.

It was finally time for the show, so we ventured to the House of Blues. Paul, a very good friend of mine, was bartending; I introduced John, mentioning that it was his first time at the club. Paul gave us wristbands to the Foundation Room, the VIP area at the House of Blues. It was very generous of him.

John was indisputably out of place, and it showed in his demeanor. It was starting to grate on my nerves. He just did not have the social graces that I'm used to. Even his Kar was beginning to look unimpressive. We sat on one of the low couches as he rambled about nothing, and then some more about nothing. *Is there something wrong with him?* I wondered. *Should I call 911?* I realized I just needed another drink.

Our fourth date was our last. I wasn't sure I wanted to see him at all, but I had tickets to hear a band we had talked about weeks before. It was at a beautiful, historic club in Los Angeles along the Miracle Mile, with a lineup of great hip-hop bands playing. Of course, the only reason I was still with John was that freaking Kar, so I insisted he drive us.

Since John was not familiar with the area, I thought it would be cool for him to see LA's history unfold from the Santa Monica coast to the Miracle Mile, a stretch of Wilshire Boulevard developed in the 1920s. What was once an unpaved farming road became one of the flashiest districts in the city, home to the entertainment industry as well as the La Brea Tar Pits, which contain skeletal remains of saber-toothed cats, mammoths and even early humans.

I was really enjoying the vibe of sharing my hometown with him. It was a Kustom Kar dream come true. We had are arms around each other; the only sounds were the rumble of the engine and the wind whooshing by. It was a punk rock version of a Harlequin romance novel: the histories of the Kar and the city, the golden silence and his manliness. Then, with a word, as we drove through Beverly Hills, the moment was gone.

"Hey, look, RO-deo," he said, pointing to a street sign.

What? I thought. Did he just say that? I laughed out loud. The romance novel flew right out the window. He thinks it's "rodeo," with horses, Wranglers and Stetsons!

"What's so funny?" he asked.

"It's Ro-DAY-o." He looked like I had just spoken Russian to him

"What?"

"Ro-DAY-o. Rodeo Drive. Not RO-deo"

"Oooh," he replied, bewildered. I laughed again.

"Have you never seen Pretty Woman with Julia Roberts? That's the street."

"Oh."

We returned to silence as we drove on to the club, but the vibe had changed. John was losing ground with me fast, and his Kar could not save him much longer.

California was in the midst of a very rainy season; in fact, it was the second rainiest in LA's history. Because John's Kar was a work in progress, it didn't do well in bad weather. We got to the venue a little early, so we hung out in the parking lot, kissing before the show. Despite his dimness, John is a kind man and a good kisser. I made an effort to put the drive behind me and focus on having a great time.

We came up for air just as it began to drizzle. Since it was close to show time, we took our places in line at the El Rey Theater. Then, it happened. The skies opened up and it began to pour. I could see by the look on his face that something was wrong. I asked if everything was okay. He said he was worried about the Kar.

> "Do you want to go?" I asked. I felt incredibly bad; I made him drive to fulfill my Kar fantasy.
>
> "Yes," he said with no hesitation. He had never been clearer about anything.

We agreed to leave the club. I was okay about missing the show. I chalked it up to a little karmic payback for my shallowness. My Jennifer-sucks-bad-behavior was the reason his Kar was out in the first place.

Even though I still respected him and his process—the amount of time and energy he painstakingly put into something he loved—that Kar was officially not cool. A little war waged in my head. *Am I actually going to say this? Did I just leave my body? Have I been taken over by an alien being?* I paused. I did not want to say what I was about to say.

"I would hate to see your Kar get damaged in the rain, so if you want, you can park it in my garage and spend the night at my house." He agreed once again with no hesitation.

When John had picked me up for our previous date, his Kar leaked a huge oil stain on the driveway. It occurred to me that if he parked in the garage overnight there would be an even bigger slick. I had visions of the Exxon Valdez, and I like my living space clean. I knew it would drive me nuts to walk through the garage day after day and see a huge oil stain in the concrete. I mentioned this to him and when we arrived at my house, he asked if I had a tarp to put down. That was polite of him, but of course I didn't, so I went in the house and grabbed some plastic garment bags from Barneys. Oh, the irony. The Foundation Room, Rodeo Drive, Barneys, and then there was John—the whole scenario was making me uncomfortable, but I was saving his Kar.

As the rain continued to pour, I was glad to be protecting his pride and joy. On the flip side, I was faced with the reality of John staying over my house. I pulled out a bottle of Patron. If I was going to spend the night with him, I was going to enjoy it.

Though it was not necessarily in my plans to have sex, we did. It was fine. He is cute, and he has a way with his hands. But in the morning, Holy Moley! What was going on in my bed? Lying there on my just-out-of-the-laundry, crisp, white sheets, I smelled the worst smell I have ever encountered! It was John, and it was coming from inside his mouth. I could have sworn something had died in there.

As he lay next to me, snoring loudly with his mouth open, I wished he were gone. My stomach sank with that sinking feeling of *How am I going to get this man out of my bed and out of my house?* AGH! I'm all about a clean mouth—I'm a twice-a-day flosser, sometimes three. As I looked at him, I realized that whatever was causing that smell had been in my mouth. If I'd known before, I would have never made out with him.

When he woke up, I asked him if I could look inside, and wow, something *had* died. His teeth were rotting, and it was bad—very, very bad. How did I not notice this before? I read him the riot act about oral hygiene, about the importance of brushing and flossing, about the fact that "oral health affects your overall health, and that your mouth is the gateway to your body" (paraphrased from a toothbrush commercial I'd seen). He was unfazed and suggested we go out for breakfast. This seemed like a good way to get him out of my house, and since I was hungry and had no food in my fridge, I agreed.

I hopped in the shower to wash his halitosis off of my body. After about five minutes, I felt a slight breeze. John had come into the bathroom. *What was he doing?* I thought. *Doesn't he have any respect for my privacy?* Of course, we'd just been naked together, but we hardly knew one another. I felt dishonored. When I emerged, he just sat there on the edge of the bathtub watching me get ready. He was so ill mannered. I didn't know what to say. He had clearly not been socialized the way I had. No car—not even a Kar was—worth this.

It was still raining, so I drove us to a local breakfast place. He tried to get a table, but I insisted we sit at the counter. I could not sit across from him and "talk." He kept trying to move closer, to lean in and make conversation, but the sound of his voice had become like nails on a chalkboard. I couldn't bear to listen to another word. We ordered, I pulled out the newspaper, and we ate in relative silence.

On the way back to my house, I had to stop by the health food store to get laundry detergent. He walked around with that oh-too-familiar Mr. Magoo look on his face. It was as though he'd never seen such a store, marveling at my choice of biodegradable, hypoallergenic detergent. "I just use Tide," he blurted. We were not on the same page. I mean, I don't care what kind of detergent he uses, but his focus was so narrow. There was nothing more to say.

In spite of the rain, when we got back to my house I made him leave. I had things to do that day, and I just didn't know what to do with him. The oil from his Kar had leaked through the Barneys bags onto my garage floor, so I helped him clean it up before he left. I gave him a polite kiss goodbye and a "See ya," hoping secretly that I wouldn't. We were just too different. I had learned a lesson in sincerity. If I had been sincere with myself from the beginning, we would have never gone past the first date. I knew he was wrong for me, but I let myself be lured by material trappings. My first attempt at "shallow dating" was a disaster, and one that I will not repeat.

I spoke to John one more time, accidentally. I thought I was calling an old friend, also named John, and got Rotten Teeth by mistake. I heard his "Hu-llo" and panicked. "Sorry, I have the wrong person," I said. But my good manners couldn't let it go—I called him back to wish him well. He was a nice guy, but not someone who could be a part of my world.

After my experience with John, I began to think more about my own powerful sense of smell. Another trip to the bookstore was in order.

Chapter Eight

The Olfactory Factor

Smells detonate softly in our memory like poignant land mines, hidden under the weedy mass of many years and experiences. Hit a tripwire of smell, and memories explode all at once. A complex vision leaps out of the undergrowth.

—Diane Ackerman, *The Natural History of Senses*

I HAVE ALWAYS been told that I'm too sensitive to smell. I can smell bad breath and body odor a mile away. I often get annoyed with people based on their smell. Sometimes I even dislike a person if their odor offends me. I pick a treadmill at the gym based on how the area smells. If the person who gets on the treadmill next to mine has a noticeable odor (perfume, cologne, body odor or, worst of all, bad breath), I will move to another. Whenever I travel by plane, I always ask the universe not to seat me next to a stinky person—one of my biggest nightmares on a long flight.

Although a hypersensitive sense of smell can be something of a curse, I have learned to embrace mine as a true blessing. Evolutionarily, smell is connected to existence: an extraordinary gift I now appreciate as a basic, primitive instinct guiding me through a modern world

Smell is one of the oldest parts of the human brain and, even more than sight and hearing, allows us to survive. In his paper "Smell and Memory," Shigeyuki Ito notes that despite our belief that "sight and hearing are the most important senses to our survival, from an evolutionary perspective smell is one of the most important."[3] Without the more than twenty thousand sensors that allow us to smell over ten thousand odors, our primitive ancestors would not have known the good berries from the bad, the rotten meat from the fresh, or been able to detect the lurking, unseen predator. In the modern world, our sense of smell allows us to tell the difference between good and spoiled milk or to detect rancid baby food. This sense is just as important today, but its usefulness may not be in the front of our minds.

Along the same lines, dating back to the ancient Greeks, the medical community has and continues to rely on smell—primarily breath—to measure health. Dr. Linus Pauling, having determined that the breath contains hundreds of substances, innovated breath testing in the 1970s. Today, from diabetes and cirrhosis to tuberculosis and cancer, doctors are increasingly able to avoid invasive testing procedures by using breath samples.[4]

Smell just as effectively plays a role in mating, though we may be less aware of its influence today. The use of scent in ritual and beautification dates back to the ancient Egyptians, spreading to Rome, Greece, Islamic cultures, and into the West. The ancient Greeks, Hindus and Chinese wore such things as castoreum (which comes from the sweat gland of beavers), a red gel pheromone of the East Asian musk deer, and civet (a viscous secretion from the Ethiopian civet cat) to attract and seduce a lover.[5]

Love potions dating back to the ancients also contained human sweat. The more outgoing cousin of the pheromone, your own essence can be the most attractive (or unattractive thing) about you. There are many examples throughout history of lovers saturating handkerchiefs, articles of clothing and even fruit with their own sweat to intoxicate lovers. In her book *The Anatomy of Love*, Dr. Helen Fisher, a leading anthropologist from Rutgers University, maintains this practice continues today: "A contemporary recipe concocted by some Caribbean immigrants to the United States reads, 'Prepare a hamburger patty. Steep it in your own sweat.

Cook. Serve to the person desired.'" I wonder if that comes with a large side of fries and a Big Gulp. Delicious!

As humans, we are all driven by our basic, primitive needs: survival and mating, as well as love, companionship and positive human connections. Our five senses are how we know whom and what attracts us, regardless of the chaos of modern life. No matter how many designer shirts or pairs of shoes you own, or what kind of car you drive, attraction is as instinctual as the need for food, water and shelter. The role of one's sense of smell is hard-wired into the brain. Helen Keller wrote, "Human odors are as varied and capable of recognition as hands and faces. The dear odors of those I love are so definite, so unmistakable, that nothing can quite obliterate them."[6]

Whether we are aware of it or not, we are attracted to people whose smell we like. This carries over from the connection to family and friends into passion and romance. In my experiences, smell has definitely been a deal breaker.

Dr. Fisher writes, "Between your eyes, within your skull, at the base of your brain, some five million olfactory neurons hang from the roof of each nasal cavity, swaying in the air currants you inhale. These nerve cells transmit messages to the part of the brain that controls your sense of smell. But they also link up with the limbic system, a group of primitive structures in the middle of your brain that govern fear, rage, hate, ecstasy, and lust. Because of this brain wiring, smells have the potential to create intense erotic feelings."[7]

If your smell is offensive to others, or you just do not have a basic chemical fit with other people, they may not respond to you. That in mind, it seems that good hygiene ranks high on the priority scale—that includes washing your body and caring for your choppers. Are you reading this, Rotten Teeth John?

Drenching yourself in manufactured fragrance may act as a Band-aid, but ultimately nature will prevail. Even if you are beautiful, a great communicator and flexible with others, at some point you still have to shower, brush and floss!

Plainly and simply, attraction comes down to having a good chemical fit with another human being. In *The Natural History of the Senses,* Diane Ackerman states, "Among far-flung tribes in a number of countries—Borneo, on the Gambia River in West Africa, in Burma, in Siberia, in India—the word 'kiss' means 'smell'; a kiss is really a prolonged smelling of one's beloved, relative or friend." As easily as it can repel, scent can bring people together.

The Survey

Armed with this new knowledge and a sense of empowerment in my special olfactory capabilities, I began to discover that others reacted as strongly to smell as I do. A waitress at a restaurant I frequent told me that she has a hard time handling all the smells she encounters, especially at work. From the people to the food, she is often overwhelmed.

On a plane, I was seated next to a man who shared my sensitivity to perfume. We both turned our overhead air vents toward an overly scented woman in front of us to divert the smell. The flight attendant told us we couldn't point them at other passengers. We both told her that the woman's perfume smell was making us sick. She left us to our devices after that.

Even psychology professionals agree that smell is a crucial part of interpersonal relationships. "Marriage counselors say that a [top] complaint from women who want to end a relationship is, 'I can't stand his smell.'"[8]

With this survey, I have done my best to represent a broad spectrum of people, with ages ranging from nineteen to sixty-two years old; an equal balance of men and women; and varied socioeconomic statuses. My goal was to open a wider dialogue about a subject that is under-discussed, and I wanted to know just how many people shared similar smell sensitivity.

I was amazed at how little people think about the connection between their senses and all that goes on around them: the connection we all have with the elements and each other. When I pointed it out to them, all of my respondents were enthusiastic about sharing their olfactory thoughts and impressions. Three young men in business suits thought it was the best pick up line they'd ever heard.

Question 1:

On a scale of 1-10, how important is smell in a relationship?

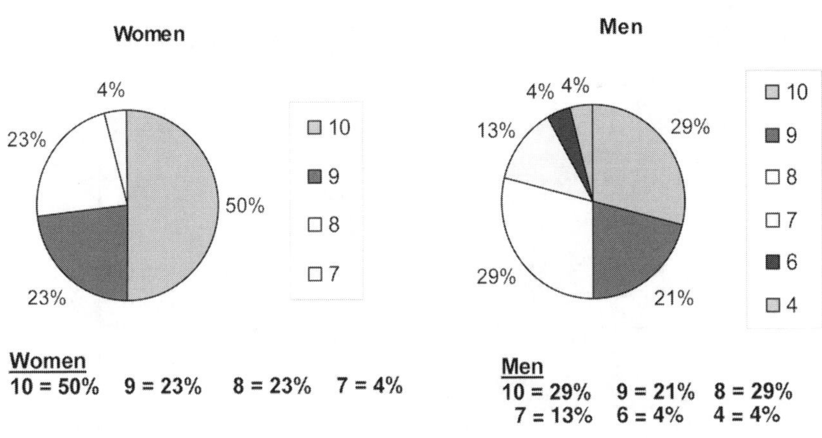

Question 2:

Has smell ever been a deal breaker?

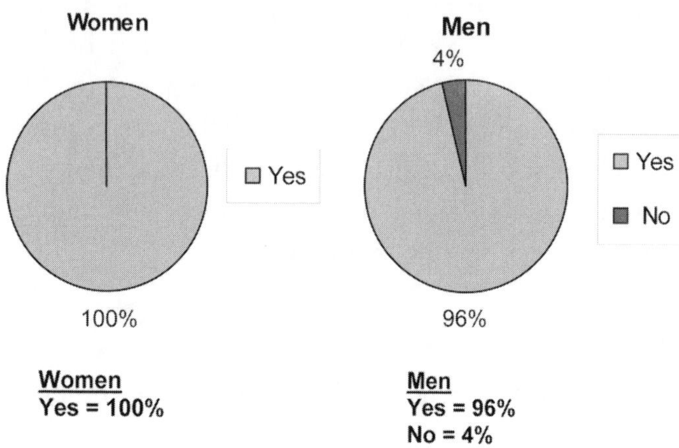

Women
Yes = 100%

Men
Yes = 96%
No = 4%

Question 3:

Have you ever had to tell your partner that he or she smells bad?

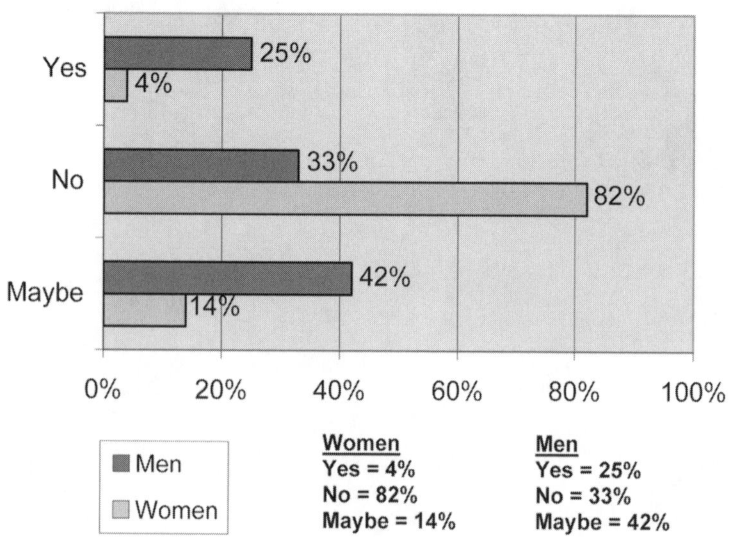

Women
Yes = 4%
No = 82%
Maybe = 14%

Men
Yes = 25%
No = 33%
Maybe = 42%

Question 4:

Do you notice how people smell in public?

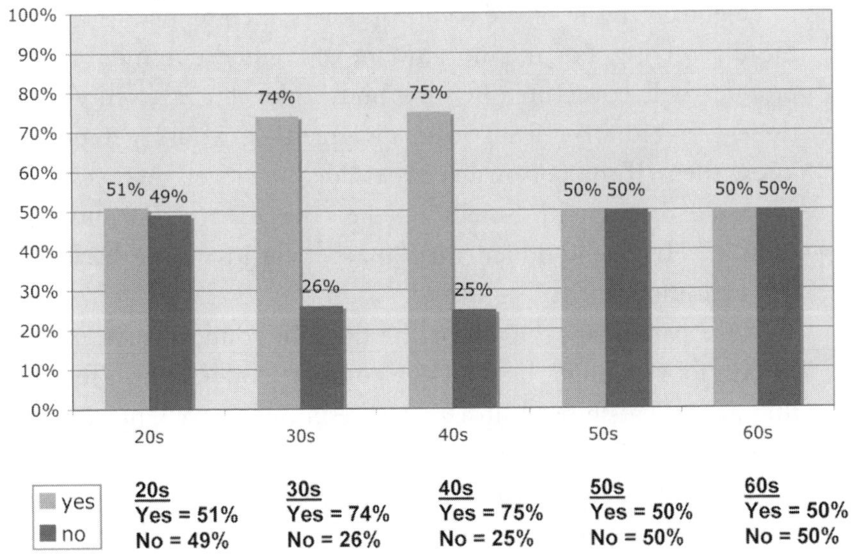

Question 5:

Would you pursue a person you find attractive, even if you don't like the way he or she smells?

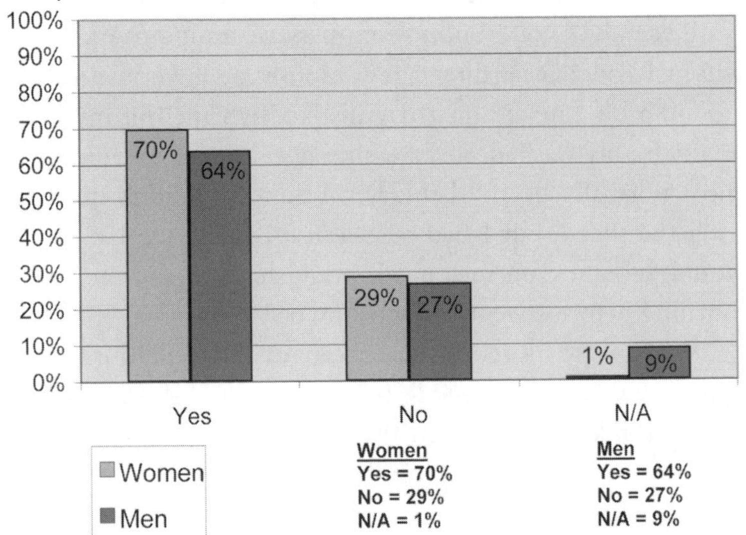

Some studies I read show that women are more attuned to their senses of smell than men are; while I found the sexes to be equally aware of the scents of others, men tended to be more forgiving. For me, no amount of scented commercial product will cover up offensive body odor, but a twenty-three-year-old man I surveyed disagreed. "I would get to know them. If the personality superseded the smell then yes, [I would date them]. Smells can be covered, a personality cannot." His friend added that "maybe she just came back from a camping trip."

One participant shared that he thought younger guys, in a quest for sex, might be willing to overlook odor, at least for the night. That showed up in other responses as well, mostly attributed to "beer goggles."

But is it alcohol, youth or hormones that make them more tolerant? As I have looked back on my own history with smell in relationships, I must admit I dated some very smelly men in my early to mid-twenties. There was the guy from Colorado, a few musicians, the rock star, and more than a couple of dirty skater boys. Bottom line: they stunk. They all had b.o., but back then, I was totally okay with that.

Recently, I got a booty-text message from a friend with whom I had a brief fling a few months ago. We just fooled around a bit, but the next day his b.o. remained in my bed, on my freshly washed, clean, white sheets. It was a Wednesday, and I normally do my laundry on Sunday. I didn't want to wash the sheets, but I had to, because I knew the b.o. smell would get stuck on me, and I would have to shower every morning before I went on with my day.

When I got his recent text message, all I could think was, *I don't want to wash the sheets.* In my twenties, I showered, but I don't think I ever washed the sheets after a b.o. boy spent the night. Is there something that changes? As we get older, do we become more discerning, more aware of what we like and don't like? Or do we just become smell snobs?

The deal breaker question made an interesting divide across age lines. While the twenties age group and folks in their fifties and sixties were split evenly on whether or not smell would cause them to end a relationship, middle-aged people were much more decisive. 75% of forty-somethings and 74% of thirty-somethings said that smell would be a deal breaker.

Question 6:
Is smell a deal breaker?

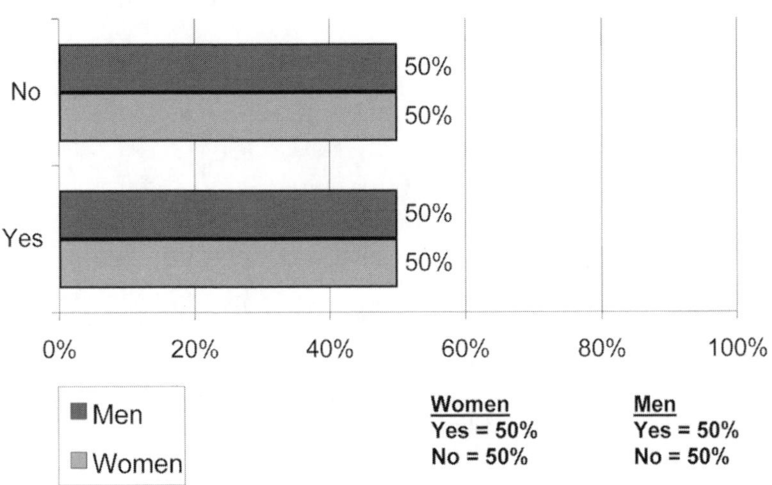

I surveyed one woman who is in her fifties and owns a perfume company. She said that even in her business, she "would not just be judgmental of smell or looks. It is more important what is on the inside of a person not on the outside."

A sixty-two-year-old gentleman I spoke with also claimed smell played no part in attraction for him. But when we came to the last question, he said something profound: "If there was a strong attraction, I think the smell may be okay." In other words, perhaps you wouldn't even be attracted to someone whose smell you don't like.

Maybe we turn into smell snobs, maybe we don't; but there is no denying that scent plays a major role in human attraction. Just as smell can evoke powerful memories, it can trigger a connection between primitively compatible people. Dr. Fisher tells us, "We each have a personal 'odor print' as distinctive as our voice, our hands and our intellect,"[9] another mystery of nature that can be acknowledged but never fully explained.

Chapter Nine

DAVE
Don't Use My Sweater Like a Towel

November 2004

DAVE AND I met at the bar of a local sushi restaurant. I was talking to him and his friends; they were a nice, funny bunch of guys. Dave immediately informed me he was the "local drunk," and I thought he was kidding. No one admits to being a drunk! I laughed, picturing him in a super hero cape with a big "D" on the back, replacing his glasses with flight goggles like some kind of alcoholic Clark Kent, swooping into bars, making merry and wreaking havoc wherever he goes. He wasn't kidding.

Dave is about my age and a VP of sales for a worldwide cosmetic company. He has a passion for deep-sea fishing, even displaying enormous stuffed fish on the walls of his home, trophies of his expeditions. Of average height and build, he is a nice looking guy. That evening, he gave me his card. We emailed for a while, developing a casual, friendly rapport. Between his business and fishing trips and my busy schedule, it took us a while before we connected again in person.

Whenever we did meet up, our dates were always last minute. One of us would call and say, "Hey, do you want to meet at The Lobster or the World?" We met at the same local places, and each time he was already out with his drinking buddies. We would have cocktails, sometimes food. Ninety-nine point nine percent of the time, we ended up at his place.

After our first "real" date—we'd preplanned our time together a few days before, which was as real a date I could have with him—we sat in my truck outside his condo, making out. I noticed he kept checking his watch.

"Do you have to be somewhere?" I asked.

"No, my ex-wife is coming over for a barbecue and will be here any minute." He didn't seem anxious or concerned.

"Oh, well, I can go. Call me later."

"No, no, it's cool," he reassured me.

I was puzzled, but we continued to make out as I wondered why he would he want me there if his ex was on her way. Then she showed up. She walked up to his door balancing a bag of groceries in one hand, ringing his buzzer with the other. Dave didn't take his leave immediately, continuing to kiss me. His ex looked somewhat agitated, pacing in front of the door with her barbecue supplies. I insisted that he go so I could get out of there and he could let her in.

He was nonchalant, but I was uncomfortable. He finally slid out of my truck without realizing that his cell phone had fallen out of his pocket and onto the floorboard. I drove away in confusion about the scene. By the time he called the next day to see if he had left his phone in my truck, he'd received about fifty calls from his drinking buddies. The "drunk phone" had been ringing off the hook; where is the "local drunk" when they need him?

At the time, I was in the online dating phase of my research for the book, making myself a human guinea pig. If the date was going badly, I would call Dave to come to my rescue. It was very cool of him—he's that kind guy. And smart, too, as I would always end up back at his place.

I had a very clear view of Dave's place in my life. He

always wanted me to spend the night, but I refused. I knew where I wanted things to go (or not go). As far as I was concerned, my time with Dave was just about drinking, hanging out and having sex—friends with benefits.

"You really don't want a boyfriend?" he would ask.

"No, I don't, not right now." I knew with absolute certainty, I didn't want the "local drunk" to be my boyfriend. A man whose judgment allowed him to make out with a woman while his ex-wife stood within view is not someone I consider boyfriend material.

He certainly had his positive qualities: he is a good man, and he was very complimentary of me and my lower parts. He gave great head. Not to be crass, but he was really into my vagina. I have never been with a man who enjoyed my vagina as much as he did. I'm talking hours a time. Needless to say, we always had fun together. But the list of reasons he could not be my boyfriend continued to grow the more time we spent together. The idea of him sitting at my family table was clearly out of the question, no matter how much he liked my vagina.

Dave's home, especially his bedroom and bathroom, was permanently a mess. Everywhere I looked, there were clothes. He traveled weekly, but still. In case you haven't noticed, I like cleanliness and order. The calcium deposits on the faucet in his shower were two inches thick. It was clear he rarely cleaned, or maybe never cleaned. Ah…more of the bachelor life!

I made it a rule to keep the lights off in the bathroom; I never touched anything but toilet paper. There was also something I did not like about the personal hygiene products he used; I think he got them from his company. I always came away with an odd, sweet smell on my skin and clothes; the odor was faint, but not a scent I wanted on me. I got much more familiar with my dry cleaner.

One night, after our usual drinks and sex, I picked up my clothes from the floor of his room and dressed to leave. It was dark and late, about 3:00 a.m. I was tired. It would have been easy to stay since it was raining out, but I didn't like to stay over: too much like girlfriend behavior. I had worn a great designer sweater, skirt and boots (actually, I never took the boots off, per his request). I drove home sleepily in the rain and went straight to bed, hanging my clothes over the chair.

In the morning, I awoke to face my jam-packed day. As I picked up my clothes from the night before, I noticed something stuck on the front of my sweater. Right in the center of the chest and all over the faux fur collar was a giant, white, crusty stain.

What is that? I thought. *How did I not see that before?* Then realization smacked me in the face. It was cum. Dave had "wiped up," using my sweater like a towel! Shock swept over me. The vision of myself behind the wheel of my truck as I drove home on the rainy streets of LA with his cum stuck on the front of my sweater still makes me laugh out loud. You'd think the faux fur would have been a dead giveaway that my sweater was not a towel. I cringed at the thought of facing my dry cleaner.

The next few times Dave and I went out, I teased him about the sweater. His friends all gave him a terrible time when they heard my story. He was embarrassed, but never really apologized or accepted the responsibility for it. He's probably still in denial.

Shortly after the sweater incident, I was on a plane to Denver. The guy next to me smelled exactly like Dave, from the products he wore to the liquor on his breath. I glanced over to discover him eating pretzels while picking his nose. It was a dreadful sight. Though obviously not the same person, this passenger with poor plane etiquette brought up some pretty negative feelings about Dave. I knew I could not be with a man who was so repulsive, and Dave was pretty darn close. As I sat there, sunlight streaming through the airplane window, flying over the Colorado Rockies, I knew I had to make a shift in our relationship when I got back to LA.

Upon my return, we had some email contact and made plans to meet for drinks. We had agreed on the when; he said he would call me with the where. The day progressed and by 6:00 p.m., he still had not called. I think it is important for people to be true to their word, and naturally, I was disappointed. If he had called to let me know he couldn't make it, there would not have been a problem.

The next day, I emailed him to see what had happened. He acted as if we'd had no plans at all, asking me, "What's new?" I told him that I found it rude, and that I would never treat a friend in such a way. He never responded. Rudeness is not a quality I admire in people, so it was fine with me.

Recently, I was out with a girlfriend at The Lobster, one of Dave's local watering holes. When I gave the bartender my credit card to open a tab, he read my name and yelled out, "Hello, Jennifer." From across the way, Dave looked up and saw me; before I could say hi, he got up from his bar stool and left. How immature. I couldn't believe he wouldn't talk to me. Many months had passed, and I was definitely over what had happened at the end of our relationship. His behavior let me know I'd made the right decision about him. I told the bartender to tell Dave I said hi the next time he was in.

Dave is a good guy, and I had no problem being friends with him. For him to turn tail and run at the sight of me showed emotional irresponsibility that I have no time or energy for. Now I associate him with that pretzel eating, nose picking guy on the airplane, his bathroom, a cape and goggles, and of course, my cum-stained sweater.

Chapter Ten

KEVIN
There Was Magic in the Kiss, But No Honor in His Words

December 2004–October 2005

THE HAIR ON a man's back is not a deal breaker, but a man that does not honor his word is. Kevin was another Match.com guy, and to the detriment of my scientific process, I quickly developed some scary, unexpected feelings for him. From our very first date in December 2004 up till our very last email contact in October 2005, I was perplexed. My emotions were all over the map. For a woman who is even-keeled and knows what she wants, the situation was more than I had bargained for. Kevin was supposed to be just part of my science project, just like the rest.

The week of our first date, I had just finished reading *Why Men Love Bitches* by Sherry Argov. While I do see eye to eye with Argov on some points, I still find it unnatural to adhere to a manual. But sticking with my mission, I would wholeheartedly follow the book's "Attraction Principles." I looked forward to seeing what would unfold as I transformed into "the bitch."

Argov's basic rules are to be "kind yet strong," a woman who "knows what she wants but won't compromise herself to get it." She also suggests one behave like a woman who is "flowery on the outside and steel on the inside." From what I read, in my opinion, she also wants you to have a dash of unavailability and aloofness in your bitch mix. She says that the men she interviewed said the "word *bitch* was synonymous with their concept of a *mental challenge.* And this characteristic, above all, they found attractive." No problem. This would be easy. I thought Kevin would be the perfect specimen.

His living situation was possibly temporary, something he disclosed from the beginning. In LA for work, he really lives about a hundred miles south of me, which made him the perfect subject for the science project—or so I thought.

We met for happy hour at a local sushi hot spot. I let him know right away that I was writing a book on human behavior, love and dating. Much to my surprise, he seemed intrigued with the idea of being a subject. Conversation flowed easily; we discovered we had past business associates in common, which was a pleasant surprise. Kevin took my hand over the dinner table to "see if there is chemistry."

There was. That first physical contact broke Attraction Principles 10 and 11 from *Why Men Love Bitches*. Right from the get go, with that simple touch, I was a rule breaker. Principle 11 states, "Being right on the verge of getting something generates a desire that has to be satisfied." She sums it up for men by adding, "You always want what you can't have." *My hands should be holding my chopsticks,* I was thinking, *not touching his over the table.*

In Principle 10, Argov says, "A woman doesn't give in easily and doesn't appear docile or submissive. It becomes more stimulating to obtain her." She goes on to say, "When a man doesn't succeed right away, he starts to crave it, it captures his interest and excites his imagination." She continues by explaining how if you are too nice, it "throws cold water on the process."

After dinner, we walked to an Irish pub to share a beer. We sat on the hard wooden bench by the window. With his arm around me and my head against his chest, I felt very relaxed and comfortable. My research was on a slippery slope.

It was a cold, damp December night; the fog had rolled in and it was getting late. Leaving the pub, we walked down Main Street, back to our cars. I asked if Kevin was cold and offered him my cashmere scarf. It's official, I was one hundred percent an Attraction Principle Breaker—my behavior was "too nice." Where were my woman of steel insides? When we got to my truck, as we were saying good night, he moved in for a kiss. At this point, having not followed Principles 10 and 11, I was moving full throttle toward breaking Principles 2 and 3.

I let him kiss me. It was one of those kisses that takes your breath away. I put my hand on the base of his neck, surprised by the hair I felt under my fingers. I thought, *I do not remember his hair being that long.* It wasn't; he is just a hairy guy. But it didn't matter. I felt we were connecting on a completely different level. And the kiss was magical.

We kissed for a good half an hour before agreeing that we should be going. He looked me straight in the eyes with his baby blues and said, "I don't just want a paragraph or page in your book; I want a whole chapter."

As I drove home, I could smell him on my skin and cashmere scarf. I liked the way he smelled on a very basic, animal level. He had that I-just-want-to-keep-smelling-you smell. It was intoxicating. I know it's corny, but even with a considerable amount of experience with men under my belt, the moment felt completely unique. The book did not have directions about this.

When I woke up, all I could think about was that kiss. There was chemistry from the moment we touched hands at the dinner table; kissing him closed the deal. The next morning I stood in my bedroom with unbrushed teeth and an unwashed face, wearing a red hooded bathrobe, with my nose stuck deep into the cashmere scarf he'd been wearing. What a bad scientist—and an absolute dork!

Having completely blown my project, I attempted to refocus. There was still a chance to follow the "bitch rules," and he still seemed like the right specimen. I blamed the kiss on the wine, but did not know what to blame my feelings on. I was in a state of denial.

The following day, the so-called sunny California skies opened violently. As the rain poured and the mountainsides slid, Kevin called me for an impromptu date, inviting me to come down to his neck of the woods for Taco Tuesday.

Why Men Love Bitches Attraction Principle 2 says, "If a woman will drop everything and drive to see a man, the man also knows that he has a 100% hold on her…A bitch is more selective about her availability. She's available sometimes; other times she's not." I wanted to follow the rules, but Taco Tuesday sounded like fun. Under normal circumstances, I would go in a second. It seemed so high maintenance to say no. *Forget the book*, I told myself. *It's raining, it sounds like fun, and I like tacos and beer.* I agreed to go.

I promised myself I would keep one of the other "bitch" commandments. The most important in my mind: I would not fool around with him. We met at his place and walked to the Mexican restaurant near his home. We laughed and talked effortlessly, enjoying each other's company. The downpour turned to drizzle, so after dinner we walked to a nearby bar that was hosting a karaoke night. We laughed the entire time. I felt remarkably relaxed. I had to remind myself, as we were sitting close, to stick to my guns. *Follow the Principles, be the bitch. This is research.*

As we walked back to his place, I was wondering, *Hmm,*

are we going to fool around? I think he was thinking the same thing. There was a hint of sexual tension as we walked closely in the drizzle. Part of me thought, *Leave when you get there. Do not go in. Don't give yourself the opportunity to get naked.* When he invited me in, I went. Getting naked overruled the "rules." So much for the bitch book.

He showed me into his living room and offered me a beer from the fridge. His roommates were gone, so we had the place to ourselves.

"I'm going to light a fire," he said, clearly trying to be romantic.

How charming. I smiled to myself as I watched him wrestle with the Duraflame log and matches. He glanced at the instructions as he put the paper-wrapped log into the fireplace. From the beginning, it had issues. It never really quite did what it was supposed to do. It took forever to light and it made weird spurting noises. I was sitting on the couch nursing a beer, watching until he joined me. He took a few large gulps of beer. That kind of hard work builds up a man's thirst.

He immediately leaned in to kiss me. The feeling from our last kiss returned—that magical, take-your-breath-away sensation. His hand went up my shirt and he asked, "Do you want to go into my bedroom?"

I said yes. He took my hand, leading the way. In minutes, I was naked except for my leather riding boots. When I reached down to take them off, he asked that I keep them on. Things were getting pretty hot and heavy when I suddenly smelled smoke. I looked up and saw it coming toward us.

"Kevin, the hallway is filling up with smoke."

Attempts at setting a romantic mood bungled, his whole house was rapidly filling with smoke. The house is fairly old, with no smoke detectors. Thank god for my acute sense of smell. He jumped up from the bed and ran down the smoky hallway. The image of this short, hairy, naked guy putting out the fire and fanning smoke was comedy at its finest. I felt like the woman he brought home to the cave; I was sure I would find a wooden club in his closet for weekends of hunting and gathering. He put out the fire without further incident and returned to me waiting in his bed, naked except for boots, where activity resumed.

The storm was still raging, accompanying us with an almost deafening pound: flashes of lightning outside, sparks flying inside. Unwanted feelings were beginning to surface. I was not ready to admit I might be interested in more than just sex and research with this man. To maintain some semblance of my project, I left very soon after we finished, driving home in the storm with his mouthwatering smell lingering on me once again.

By this time, I had also broken Principle 21: "If a man has to wait before he sleeps with a woman, he'll not only perceive her as more beautiful, he'll also take time to appreciate who she is." Argov thinks that actually it is best to stay "platonic for the first month."

We were both in and out of town a lot in the following weeks, so it gave me some time to sort through my feelings and own up to the fact that I had completely blown my science project. It was not until mid-January that we were able to configure our schedules to see one another again.

It gave me time to think. Unfortunately, I thought about him way more than I wanted to. I'm normally not so affected by men early in relationships. Returning to the project, I began to research the chemical reactions in the human body after sex, during the phases of like, love and lust. I discovered that as the chemicals get flowing, they become like powerful drugs. I was officially an addict: addicted to Kevin, my science project gone awry.

I knew in my heart that he was not "the one," but I kept my options open. The reactions of my body and mind gave me the illusion there was hope for the future. It was quite interesting that his height or hairiness never became an issue. It didn't bother me when I used the masking tape lint brush to capture the body hair he left behind in my bed. Something bigger seemed to be going on. Otherwise, I would have never let him in my bedroom.

Inviting a man into my own bed is a big deal for me. There must be some sort of history or a deeper connection. I felt that with Kevin. But for all the times we "slept" together, we only woke up together once.

It was an enjoyable morning; we lounged, fooled around and hung out in bed, laughing and talking. But when I suggested we go out for breakfast, there was hesitation.

> "I don't have breakfast clothes," he said, as if that were an obvious reason not to eat.
>
> "What? What do you mean?"
>
> "I only have the clothes I wore last night. I can't go to breakfast in those. At breakfast you wear shorts and flip-flops."

Did he read that in *Men's Health*? It wasn't like he had been wearing a tuxedo. It made no sense to me, but he would not give in. Maybe that was his excuse to leave, but I'll never know. Perhaps he feared going to another level of intimacy—breakfast is *so* intimate—or he wanted to avoid any further connection with me. As much as I liked him, this moment was a red flag.

Despite the warning signs, I felt we were growing closer

as we continued to get to know each other. One evening we were having sex, and I could really feel myself falling for him, figuratively and literally, despite the feeling in my gut. During our passionate, rough-and-tumble activities, I fell right out of my bed, buck naked, flat on my ass on the bamboo floor. It was not one of my more graceful moments. I laughed, struggling to remain sexy and composed. As I got back into bed, I said with a smile, "You pushed me."

"No, I didn't. You fell out." It became our joke.

That moment of clumsiness allowed me to drop another wall: I decided to let him cum in me. I knew we were both clean; I am on the pill and have been told by my doctor that I cannot get pregnant. Most of all, I trusted him. It was a huge step—something very intimate. I don't let just any man do that. Based on his past behavior, it was not a surprise that he left as soon as we finished having sex. Maybe he didn't have "breakfast clothes."

Alone there in my bed, the whole relationship felt empty, like a sham. I went to sleep thinking that it was a mistake to make myself that vulnerable to him. The next morning, I went to the bathroom to pee and I noticed a terrible smell coming from down there. The smell of his cum inside me was pungent and I did not like it. My body seemed to be telling me something on a protective, animalistic level. Was it telling me not to get close to this person? Or was I reading too much into the whole thing? I hoped the scent of "our mix" was just a fluke, a one-time bad reaction. But even after I showered, the smell lingered, or at least it did in my mind.

I rarely skipped yoga, but that morning, I was convinced that my yoga teacher, who knows me very well, would notice the smell when he came over to adjust me. I stayed at home most of the day, working from my home office, in fear that my smell would offend somebody. Later that evening, I had a Brazilian wax appointment. I went even though I felt smelly. As I lay on the table with my legs spread wide and hot wax in my butt, I told Maria, the aesthetician, my stinky-sperm story.

"Do I smell bad?" I asked her bluntly.

"No, sweetie."

"Maria, I need you to be completely, one hundred percent honest with me. I don't know if we mix. This is vital to the future of my relationship with this man. Be frank. Tell me the truth."

"No, sweetie, you smell fine," she repeated in her thick Russian accent.

"Are you sure? What if I'm falling for someone and can't handle the way we mix? We had such great sex, and I love the way he smells otherwise. I enjoy giving him head; his smell was never an issue before. This is a whole new territory for me."

Maria's reassurance that I was odorless made me feel so much better. Although the fact that she made her living sticking her nose in ladies' nether regions made me wonder if her sense of smell had dulled over the years. Or maybe she was just being nice.

I decided that it must have been a fluke. *The next time we have sex*, I thought, *I'll let him cum in me and see what happens. If I'm uncomfortable with the smell, I will have to really give this relationship some serious thought*. There was no way I could be with a man whose semen forced me into hibernation.

We went out shortly after the stinky sperm incident. We had a great night as always, ending up back in my bed. Once again, we had sex. Back in scientist mode, I let him cum in me, almost afraid of the outcome. Now, more than just my dating life, my vagina had become part of the science project.

History repeated itself: he did not stay the night, and I was left with that same empty feeling. I was also a little relieved. I like morning sex and, if I did smell bad, I would have been uncomfortable having him there. In the morning, as I made my way to the bathroom, I kept my fingers crossed for a positive result.

Sure enough, I stank. It was the same exact smell as before. *How can this be?* I wondered. *Is it something he eats? Something I eat? The combo? It must just be our "mix."* Of course, I realized that he could not cum in me anymore—this man I really liked, this man I was possibly falling for.

We had to have "the discussion." How do you tell someone his cum makes you stink? I let him know that when he came in me it made me uncomfortable on an animal level, and that it would not be a good idea for him to "do it in me anymore." He just stared at me blankly, saying nothing. I should have said, "For twenty-four hours after you cum in me, I smell like a rotten fish market." Maybe that would have gotten a reaction.

The stinky sperm moment passed, but still I had strong, unexplainable feelings for Kevin. I would always look forward to seeing him and we always had fun together. There was so much to like: he called if he was running late, opened car doors, never let me pay for meals or drinks, and always a nice gesture, he took my hand when we walked down the street. At restaurants, he sat next to me instead of across. His behavior was warm, loving and inviting. Except for the stinky sperm, and the fact that he bolted immediately after sex, he was almost perfect. Almost.

He was also hard to pin down. It was like a Mexican hat

dance from the beginning, a struggle between two very independent, strong-minded people. We continued to see one another when our schedules allowed. I am a busy woman with a thriving career and my own ideas about what a relationship is. Kevin is equally driven in his own world. The attraction was there, but his behavior was utterly confusing to me. One minute he would tell me that he pines for me if he goes too long without seeing me; the next, he was taking weeks to follow up on an email or text message. I didn't anticipate wanting him to be my boyfriend. Defensively, I began to mirror his behavior. The more emotionally unavailable he was, the more emotionally unavailable I became.

But did I want a science project or a boyfriend? I am thankful his bad behavior forced me to look at my own reality, to think about what I really want and what am I willing to tolerate. After twenty-seven years of dating, it was an epiphany.

"I choose love." I wrote those words on a small, blue Post-it and taped it in the top drawer of my bathroom cabinet on March 30, 2005. Based on this revelation, I called him and said, "I do not think we should see each other anymore." We agreed we would be better as friends.

Even though I'd said the words, I was still perplexed and sad. I knew he wasn't good for me, but I missed him—or at least the idea of him. I went to yoga the next morning hoping it would take my mind off him, but it didn't. In downward dog (butt in the air, arms stretched out, feet planted firmly in the mat), I held back my tears.

I take full responsibility for choosing the men I date and sleep with. I could see that in my usual pattern, I was attracting a type of man that is unhealthy for me. My gut was telling me one thing and my heart another.

Kevin—Another Try
May 11, 2005

Three months passed, and though Kevin and I hadn't been seeing each other, I was still thinking about him. I'm not sleeping with him, I thought. I haven't seen him in a long time. I can't blame it on a chemical response in my body. Why do I keep thinking about him? That is when I opened Pandora's Box. I would rather crack something open and take the consequences than deal with stagnancy.

"Life is short," an older woman said to me at the gym, listening to the bad news on the locker room TV. "You could choke to death on a string bean at lunch." I replied, "That is why it is important to LIVE life." We both nodded in agreement.

The one-year anniversary of the science project was approaching and I decided to call Kevin to see if there was still something there. I spilled my guts out to him during our phone conversation, laying it all on the line. "I'm going out of town this week," he said. "I'll call you when I get back."

But he never called me back. Whether he lied, forgot, didn't care or just got scared, whatever his reasons, it felt like the ultimate slap in the face. *Kevin,* I felt like telling him, *you don't keep your word. I put my cards out on the table with you during that phone call and you took it for granted.* Feeling hurt and disrespected, I sent him an email:

> I have a motto that evolved out of many years of running my own business: As long as you are honest, organized and on time, you will be fine. I live by these words and it is that just plain and simple. It is about keeping your word.

I wanted him to know exactly where I was coming from.

I was surprised to hear back from him, and even more surprised by his positive reaction. I decided to email him a few pages of the book from his chapter. His response was, again, inappropriately positive. *Did he read what I sent?* It was just the kind of head-in-the-sand reaction I had come to expect from him. I basically called him a liar, and he conveniently ignored it, asking to read more. This guy was beyond confusing. No wonder I was perplexed. He only seemed to be "available" when reading about himself or challenged. Then he would disappear again.

After a round of unanswered text messages and voice mails, I emailed him an excerpt of his chapter that described our first date. Once again he resurfaced, asking for more pages. I'm sure his ego was inflated by what I wrote. I suggested we meet for drinks to talk about things. He agreed, sending me the following text message:

From Kevin:
text message sent 8:17 p.m., June 12, 2005

good idea I was gonna suggest we meet so ud figure it out in person.

I'd figure it out? All I knew was that nothing had changed with him. I opened my heart and he ignored it.

My first instinct was to pick up the phone and let him know exactly how I felt—crack it open. What if I choke on that string bean? He is remarkably accomplished at avoiding situations that make him uncomfortable. We all have emotional issues to work through, I accept that. But in any relationship, the level of communication needs to be open, fluid. Still, I opted to wait until our date.

That night, I lay in bed reading *If the Buddha Dated* by Charlotte Kasl, PhD. I was startled by a shrill warning sound coming from the TV in the background. I thought it was an Amber Alert, but then a voice took over where the siren left off, informing me that there had been an earthquake that could cause a tsunami. The voice said to evacuate. Heart racing, I called my mother. After the tsunamis in Asia earlier in the year, the thought of widespread destruction was terrifying. I live on the coast and would be swept up by the ocean. What if this was the Big One I have heard about my entire life? What if the shoe and handbag collection I promised my nieces was lost at sea? What if this was my string bean?

My mother said to come to their house. My father suggested I drive five miles east, sit in a bar, and have cocktails for a few hours. If nothing happened, I should go home. Calmed by Weather Channel reports that "scientists were divided on the likelihood of a tsunami," I opted to stay put, returning to the book, relieved I did not have to pack my wardrobe into my car and head for higher ground. But what I read hit me like an earthquake.

> When we create a mindful, loving personal connection with another, and we are sexually attracted to that person, our bodies produce the hormone oxytocin, which contributes to feelings of intense closeness, trust, and sensual feelings. Incidentally, oxytocin is the same hormone that is secreted when a mother nurses her baby. According to Pearsall, 'it's the neurochemical of intimate connection that also helps balance the immune system.' It takes considerable periods of time in a growing, reciprocal, loving union for our bodies to stop creating an epinephrine high and secrete oxytocin instead, which means that many people never have the experience of intense intimacy[10].

I had read about neurochemicals in my earlier research,

but something about this detailed description of its effects hit home.

Kevin and I had a very intimate connection from the get go. Every time we had sex, all that epinephrine was running through my blood stream. When he would leave, it brought up all kinds of trust issues. My body, on a chemical level, needed and expected closeness. His behavior was playing against that biological connection. I think that reaction manifested itself many times—even after we kissed. Eventually I got to the end of my rope. *I cannot see this man any longer*, I realized. My body, mind and spirit were in a state of chemical chaos.

Dr. Kasl goes on to say, "Your thoughts, feelings, cells, hormones, glands, consciousness, tenderness, compassion, sexuality and integrity are like the pieces in a kaleidoscope interacting with each other, creating the design of who we are and how we feel. The more they come together as an integrated whole, the more we can trust our attraction." The bottom line was, I had never been able to trust my attraction to him.

Kevin called me the day of our date to tell me he was fighting off a cold, but he still wanted to get together. I suggested we meet at the Canal Club for happy hour. I was a little nervous about seeing him. Our last date had been over two months before. I got there early to have a glass of wine, but I still felt on edge.

Right on time, he came in from behind me and sat down on the bar stool next to mine. He looked cute, and as much as I did not want to be, I still found myself attracted to him. I was determined to keep the conversation light and fluffy. We talked about the general stuff: work, family, the usual. Conversation turned pretty quickly to the book and the rough pages of the chapter I emailed him.

"I was surprised by the title," he said. "I don't understand the 'honor in his words' part. I feel like I have been honest with you."

Amazing, I thought. He did read it.

"Kevin, when I spilled my guts to you on the phone, I felt like I was throwing myself in front of a train. That was out of context for me." What I didn't say was that when he didn't call, it was like the train had run over me, leaving me for dead. "Not calling when you say you will is not walking your talk. Don't say you're going to do something and not do it."

"Oh." He paused for a moment. We were picking over sushi and chicken satay. "When you told me all of that, I was seeing someone else."

"Why didn't you tell me? I wouldn't have minded." He didn't have an answer. "Are you still seeing her?"

"No, we both decided there were no sparks." I sat there wondering, Do we have sparks? I decided not to ask.

We finished dinner and walked outside. It was a beautiful summer night at the beach; the sun was just beginning to set. I really wanted to hang out some more, take a walk along the beach, but since he was not feeling well, I walked him to his car. We hugged good night.

I took that walk anyway, to clear my head. I realized I need a man who will step up to the plate and let me know how he feels. I will be forty years old in November, as I pointed out to him at dinner. It was my subtle way of telling him, of telling myself, that I was done playing games.

I called Kevin when I got home to thank him again for

dinner. Soon after, I heard my cell phone ring. I hoped it was him, calling me back with some kind of true confession (so Nancy Drew of me), but I didn't get to the phone in time. I checked to see who called, and to my great surprise, it was Damon! I had not talked with him since I'd been snowboarding in Steamboat three months before; since then we had only had email and text message contact. It was good to hear his voice, and his timing was truly kismet.

Damon is the kind of man you can bring to the family table. He is trustworthy and knows how to communicate honestly. I have never wondered if he likes me. I have always known exactly where we stand with each other—no games. All this rang in my brain as I listened to Damon's deep voice. There are men out there who will be better choices for me, though I still find myself hung up on Kevin.

I lay awake that night processing my unfulfilled feelings and many unanswered questions. There was so much I need to say, so much to figure out. I always ask the questions I need answered, but with him, I walked on eggshells. It was so unhealthy, so completely out of my character. In the dark of my room, I realized I never felt I could ask him what I needed to ask in fear of the answer—or in his case, non-answer.

I flashed back to when I was about twenty-three and feeling sad. I remember very vividly writing about fate and destiny: "Do we control our destiny or does destiny control us?" That thought evolved into the present as I grabbed a pen and pad from my night table and wrote, "The hand of fate cannot be forced."

My grandmother, a huge fatalist, always used to say, "What will be, will be." I believe that is true. What goes on in the dating process and the search for love, the ultimate chemical reaction between people, cannot be forced. It's hard when your heart gets stuck on an idea or when you feel you have a real connection with somebody. But if you have to over-think something, you are trying too hard. If things aren't happening organically, when you find yourself pushing, you are on the wrong path.

That's not what will be, will be. You're trying to make it be. But as exhausting as it is, there is no bad experience. Even when it's hard, you need to go through it to get to the next place. As only humans can, we complicate things with dialogue that gets going in our heads. It's really all very simple at the end of the day, but all of our garbage goes into it and we can easily be confused. Trying to be present, as hard as it is, is really all you can do. If you are happy with yourself, you're going to be happy with others.

Kevin has become the poster boy for the multitude of ways a relationship can go wrong. I even wrote him my first "Dear John" letter. We were never able to give one another what we wanted. I know what I need to be happy, and I won't settle for someone who gives just enough to keep me wanting more. I would rather be single. I admit I am as responsible as he is, but in the end, I gave it an honest Girl Scout effort.

I have gone from a state of perplexity to clarity. I am no longer in the dark, wondering where we stand. There has been sadness, but I know that time is healing. By moving on, I am making room in my life for a healthy relationship—and for love.

In *Why We Love*, Dr. Helen E. Fisher says, "Love is one of the most powerful driving forces on earth." I believe this is true. So why do we continue to invest time and energy in people who are unavailable and incapable of nurturing our love? In a moment of true synchronicity, the following evening after I read those words, I was watching *Six Feet Under*. One character said to another, "Love is not something you feel, it is something you do. And if the person you are with does not want it, you know what? Do yourself a favor and save it for someone who does."

Chapter Eleven

Like, Love or Dopamine

'What is love?' Shakespeare mused. The Great bard was not the first to ask. I suspect our ancestors pondered this question a million years ago as they sat around their campfires of lay and watched the stars.
—Helen Fisher, Why We Love

IT WAS ANOTHER picturesque summer night along the Southern California coast. I sat at the bar of the Mercedes Grill, one of my favorite work spots, while listening to freshly downloaded hip-hop on my iPod and reading over a massive stack of notes about the chemical reactions that occur during the various stages of human love. A man sporting a huge, unkempt mustache and tacky, black rayon Hawaiian shirt sat down next to me and asked what I was doing. He was somewhat gruff—certainly no Johnny Depp. But not wanting to be rude, I answered him.

"It's research for a book I'm writing. This chapter is about how chemicals in the body are released during each stage of lust, attraction and love. Such as dopamine, phenylethylamine, testosterone, oxytocin—"

He cut me off impolitely and said, "Love does not involve chemicals. Testosterone is the only chemical involved with love." Okay. Whatever you say, mustache guy. I began to explain further, but he cut me off again, resolute that I was incorrect.

His opposition shocked me. In front of me were numerous articles and two books by Helen Fisher, PhD that reported otherwise, but this man insisted he was right. There were no ands, ifs or buts as far as he was concerned. Not only was his protest puzzling, his closed-mindedness was uneducated.

It was turning into an argument, so I moved to a stool at the other end of the bar.

Months later, I attended a family wedding; all my nieces and nephews were there. I was bowled over at how much they all had grown since I last saw them. My niece Megan had gone from a kid to a teenager seemingly overnight.

We were sitting around talking when the subject of puberty and hormones came up: cone tits, pubic hair, the works. Listening to what they knew, which was very little, I realized that many of us are still operating with the same information about hormones that we got (or did not get) when we were eleven. I thought of mustache guy, who was no more informed than my eleven-year-old niece, or as I was up until a few months ago.

This is not the stuff you learn in health class. Hopefully after you read this you won't think love is just about testosterone, but will have a better understanding of how hormones influence our brains and bodies. The next time you have that I-just-can't-get-you-off-my-mind feeling, you'll know it's the chemical network built into your DNA.

The truth is, falling in love is equivalent to being on drugs, and I am talking hard drugs. As Dr. Susan Block says, "Falling in love is a natural high finer and smoother than anything you could inject, smoke, snort, drink or swallow. Of course, love is not something you can pick up at the pharmacy or even on the black market. It strikes you like a mystical gift from god, or a practical joke from tricky, fickle old Hot Mama Nature. Then it stirs up the euphoric, love-juicy chemical goo that permeates your cells, creating a place within you where hormones meet holiness, wildflowers bloom, angels dance, and the city never sleeps."[11]

Hormones 101

At any given time, hundreds of chemicals course through our bodies and affect our behavior. They control everything from eating and sleeping to laughing and crying. Hormones are chemicals that act as messengers, bringing information to and from cells. Neurotransmitters are chemicals that send electric impulses between the neurons of the brain to other cells in the body.

Androgens and **Estrogens** are steroid groups found in both genders that act primarily as sex hormones. While men and women produce hormones from both groups, women have higher quantities of estrogens, while men have higher quantities of androgens. Testosterone is a member of the androgen group. It enhances libido, increases energy and buffers the immune system in both men and women. Estradiol, estriol, and estrone are estrogens produced when androgens synthesize with enzymes. These hormones, excreted by the reproductive organs (ovaries in women and testes in men) and the brain, intensify the drive to mate and procreate.

Dopamine is a neurotransmitter often called the pleasure/pain chemical. It is closely associated with sexual desire and addiction. Dopamine also affects the brain functions of movement and emotional reaction. Dopamine increases sex drive by boosting the release of testosterone. According to Helen Fisher, "It's the neurochemical dopamine in particular that allows us to maintain romantic love's unique, intoxicating properties, even as we tread water in the tranquil sea of long term attachment."[12]

Norepinephrine is a neurotransmitter that also acts as a stress hormone, affecting attention span and impulsiveness.

When combined with epinephrine, it is associated with fight-or-flight responses.

Oxytocin is a peptide of nine amino acids that was, until recently, thought only to induce labor, lactation and bonding between a mother and child. Now it is believed to be instrumental in attachment between romantic partners as well. It is secreted by the pituitary gland, stimulating the brain and reproductive glands of both men and women.

Dr. Theresa Crenshaw, in her book *The Alchemy of Love and Lust*, calls oxytocin "hormonal superglue." When loved ones come in physical contact—from family and friends to romantic partners—oxytocin is released, connecting people with every caress or cuddle. As the initial lust-inducing chemicals wear off, oxytocin keeps us together.

Phenylethylamine is a neurotransmitter and naturally occurring amphetamine that stimulates increasing feelings of excitement. "This violent emotional disturbance that we call infatuation (or attraction) may begin with a small molecule called phenylethylamine, or PEA. Known as the excitant amine, PEA is a substance in the brain that causes feelings of elation, exhilaration, and euphoria."[13] PEA transports via neurons through all sectors of the brain giving the sensation of overwhelming joy.

Pheromones are naturally occurring chemicals believed to be produced by the apocrine glands and transmitted by scent between animals of the same species, including humans. This allows a subliminal communication of bonding and attraction.

Serotonin is another neurotransmitter that affects mood and attraction, but this one behaves a little differently. High levels of serotonin are associated with happy feelings, while low levels are believed to cause depression, affecting appetite and sex drive. Dr. Fisher explains, "As well as high [levels of] dopamine and norepinephrine, romantic love is characterized by low serotonin. Low serotonin would explain the obsessive thinking attached to romantic love."[14]

Vasopressin is the male counterpart to oxytocin, produced by the brain as well as male and female sex organs. Both chemicals are released during sexual stimulation and are believed to trigger feelings of comfort and trust. "At orgasm, vasopressin levels dramatically increase in men, oxytocin levels rise in women."[15]

Stages of Love

Along with a team of top scientists, Dr. Fisher has done vast amounts of research on love and human chemistry. By performing MRI brain scans on people who are deeply in love, she and her colleagues established that when you fall in love, certain parts of the brain are flooded with blood, proving that passion is hardwired into our brains by millions of years of evolution.

Modern human romance can feel like a rollercoaster ride. When in love, feelings triggered by these chemicals "have the ability to override the part of your brain that governs rational thought," Fisher explains. It is entirely chemical, and often acts like addiction. "Virtually all drugs of abuse affect a single pathway in the brain…activated by dopamine. Romantic love stimulates the same pathway with the same chemical."[16] Therefore, when our bodies and brains go for that ride, we want to go again and again.

The first stage of love is lust, according to Dr. Fisher, which is marked by high levels of testosterone and estrogen in both sexes. "Lust evolved to get you out looking for anything."[17] Our bodies' natural drives to mate and procreate send us out on the prowl.

Following lust is the romantic love stage. Fisher explains that romantic love is "not an emotion. Rather it's a motivation system. It's a drive. It's part of the reward system of the brain." Dopamine and PEA levels begin to rise, increasing our excitement about the person we desire. "Sex elevates testosterone levels which then rev up the dopamine." The reason we feel elated when we think of our new love, and on the flip side, depressed when they are not around, is the result of chemical spikes of dopamine and PEA in our brains. "No wonder lovers can stay awake all night talking and caressing. No wonder they become so absentminded, so giddy, so optimistic, so gregarious, so full of life. Naturally occurring amphetamines have pooled in the emotional centers of their brains; they are high on speed."[18]

As a relationship progresses, dopamine levels begin to taper off, that I-need-to-get-my-hands-on-your-body-this-very-second feeling becomes less intense, and romance moves into attachment, Fisher's third stage of love. That's where oxytocin and vasopressin take over, creating "the sense of calm, peace and stability one feels with a long-term partner."

Oxytocin and vasopressin are known as the "cuddle chemicals." Oxytocin is released during childbirth and aids lactation in women, but it is also emitted by both men and women during orgasm. Vasopressin, the male bonding chemical, is released through the kidneys. Both aid a long-term connection between romantic partners for the care and nurture of children. According to *Psychology Today*, "Warm and fuzzy though they make us feel, these hormones can't match dopamine's edgy high."[19]

Monogamy

"Only about 3% of mammals are monogamous, mating and bonding with one partner for life…scientists tell us humans are not one of these naturally monogamous mammals."[20] Monogamy in humans is primarily a social construct. According to research, chemicals that keep the relationship exciting, like dopamine and PEA, only remain in the body for three to five years of a relationship, "long enough to procreate and then protect the child during early years of life."[21] So what hope do we have of achieving a lasting, loving relationship? Dr. Fisher reassures us that in her studies, "This yearning for emotional togetherness far surpasses the desire for mere sexual release." But how long it will last is conjecture. Dr. Fisher goes on to say, "It seems to be the destiny of humankind that we are *neurologically* able to love more than one person at a time. You can feel profound attachment for a long-term spouse, while you feel romantic passion for someone in the office or your social circle, while you feel the sex drive as you read a book, watch a movie, or do something else unrelated to either partner. You can even swing from one feeling to another."[22]

Many theories exist as to why long-term loving relationships work, despite our seeming chemical disadvantage. The psychiatric community is divided as to whether these powerful chemicals are triggered by emotion or our emotions trigger the chemicals. Humans, unlike most animals, have the ability to consciously override the neurological and chemically enhanced dance in our heads. That is why we can end a relationship with someone we are "in love" with, or begin one with someone who is completely wrong for us.

We also have powers of reason and decision-making that

can let us choose a life direction that is right for us. Psychologist Robert Sternberg "divides love into three basic ingredients: passion, intimacy and decision/commitment."[23] Our ability to decide what path to take allows us the possibility of a lifetime connection with another person. I believe we all have the desire for a lasting relationship built into our makeup. Mother Nature plays her part and we play ours. "Nature isn't tidy; she likes options," Dr. Fisher adds, "and there is no definite relationship between neurotransmitters of romance and the hormones of attachment. As should be said of all these chemical interactions: it depends."[24]

Why We Love Love

Everywhere you turn, love is held up as the ideal of emotional expression. Whether it's a play about the joy of discovering a new romantic partner or a country song mourning the loss of love gone bad, there is nothing so perfect, so painful as love. There is something deep within us that makes us crave that ultimate connection, and we will do all within our power to make it last.

Building families and ensuring the continuation of the genetic line may be the inherent goal of coupling, but the promise of love's highs keeps us motivated to find a partner with whom we connect, despite the lows we know can be just around the corner. The desire for love is as much a part of our inherited makeup as the color of our eyes. It's traceable through history in our art, poetry and the stories passed down through the generations. From the beginning of time, we have searched for love, and we will continue to do so.

"Westerners adore love. We symbolize it, study it, worship it, idealize it, applaud it, fear it, envy it, live for it, and die for it. Love is many things to many people. But love is common to all people everywhere and associated with tiny molecules that reside at the nerve endings in the emotional centers of the brain, then love is also primitive."[25] Nature provides us with the tools to start, develop and sustain loving, lasting and connected relationships. We just have to choose to surrender and make the leap.

Chapter Twelve

SCOTT
Burning Bridges

January 2005

I HAVE KNOWN Scott for more than ten years. We met at a cowboy bar in Jackson Hole, Wyoming at Christmastime in the early nineties. At that time, Jackson Hole was not quite the celebrity enclave it is today—no Four Seasons, no multi-million dollar homes—just a little ranch town with some of the best skiing, snowboarding and deep powder in the Rockies. Snowed in, with all my clothing and snowboarding equipment stuck at the Denver airport, I only had a backpack with toiletries and the clothes I wore on the plane.

Not dressed for such bad weather, my goal was to escape the snowstorm by ducking into the first place I found for dinner and a cocktail. I ended up in a local saloon, sitting at the bar surrounded by real cowboys in big brimmed hats, big belt buckles, blue jeans, Western-style snap-front shirts, flannels and huge moustaches. I think I even counted a few heavily waxed, creatively curled handlebar 'staches. One of the only women there, and looking very much the tourist, I was being hit on from all sides within minutes.

I was feeling very uncomfortable. The last thing I wanted was one of those cowboy hats poking me in the eye. Scott, in jeans and a sweater, clearly not one of the local cowboys, must have sensed my discomfort from across the room. He came to my rescue.

He sat down and introduced himself. Scott was a handsome guy, about my age, with dirty blonde hair and brown eyes. He said he was from Seattle and was watching a friend's home for the holidays. We had effortless conversation, hitting it off right away. Since we were snowed in, he invited me to his friend's house for the night. Glad for the company, and thankful to be rescued, I went.

It was just Scott, his dog and me, but I felt very safe in the strangers' house. There was no sex—I am not sure if we even kissed—but we spent every night in the same bed. All three days I was in Jackson, I had fun just hanging out in the town, enjoying the beauty of the mountains, even with all my stuff still stuck in Denver.

Scott and I had a memorable time; I felt very comfortable with him; there was no pressure to be more than friends. Being snowed in turned out to be a tranquil experience. The bonus of sharing it with a cute guy was my consolation prize for not being able to get on the mountain. Finally, on my last day, the snow relented enough to allow my things to be flown in. Scott was kind enough to drive me to the airport to pick up my gear. I was finally able to get on the mountain and ride.

Once the storm subsided, we both went back to our home states and continued to keep in touch. I sent him samples from my clothing line. He kept me posted on his work within the music industry. We remained long-distance friends for a long time.

Years later, I was in Seattle documenting the art and lives of homeless and runaway youth for an Internet art project. I met Scott for drinks the first night I was in town. We both got pretty drunk, though maybe I was worse off than him. Later that night, we went back to my hotel room and had sex. I barely remember it, but I do remember that when I woke up the next morning, he was gone. No note, no message at the front desk, no nothing. I was shocked. In my mind, we were friends with a history. Sex or no sex, this was not "friendly" behavior. It was disrespectful, and certainly not how one treats a friend.

Scott had disappeared, but what remained was the smell—like dirty, old, stinky socks—and now it was on me. It was so odd, and I could only speculate that it came from him, but he was gone, so I couldn't ask him. I was not about to call him—what would I say? "Hello, Scott? It's Jennifer. Remember me? You left me in bed after a night of sex with no note or message, but there is this vile, awful smell stuck on me. Is it yours?"

It took me a while to get the smell off my body and out of my hair. Feeling hurt and used, I went back to LA without an explanation. About a week passed with no word at all from Scott. As I have mentioned before, I was raised to be a lady. I would never burn a bridge. You never know how a person may affect your life in the future. Whether in your personal life or in business dealings, it's better to leave a bad or uncomfortable situation, taking the high road with grace, keeping the bridge intact.

I sent Scott a letter. I was very polite, though I would have been justified telling him off. He was in the music industry, and during that time I was doing a lot of private label and band merchandise. I knew that one day our paths would cross again; it was just a matter of time. The letter said, "I don't know what happened to you, but I'm sure we'll see each other out on the path. Good luck with all." I meant it.

About a year later, I was sitting in my company's exhibitor space at North by Northwest, a now defunct music conference in Portland, Oregon, when our paths indeed crossed again. Surrounded by clients, industry associates and friends I have done business with for many years, I was in my element. Scott walked nonchalantly toward the booth, pausing for a moment. Then came the recognition. His eyes said, *Oh god, that's Jennifer.* He stood there quietly for a couple of minutes, and seeing I was too busy to talk, he moved on without a word. Later that day, when things slowed down, he returned.

> "Hi," he said. "Listen, I'm really sorry about that night in Seattle."
>
> "It's okay. We all do what we do," I reassured him. "It's not a big deal."
>
> Nervously he said, "It's just that I was going through a lot of stuff with the girl I was living with, and..." I didn't care about his explanation.
>
> "It doesn't matter. It's cool, really. I'm over it. Here. Take my card. Call me the next time you're in town."

I really meant what I said. Time had passed; I said what I needed to say in the letter. Since I had taken the high road, I was able to be in that moment, completely secure in my own behavior and actions.

We have casually kept in touch ever since. He currently works for a not-for-profit organization created by a pop music icon, and is in and out of LA frequently. Our meetings over the years have always been very casual, spontaneous and brief. One night we even met for drinks and had a very pleasant time.

Then one random rainy day, completely out of the blue, I got the raunchiest, most sexually blunt email I have ever received. It was from Scott. He was in LA for business, and wanted to meet for drinks—and sex. He let me know, in no uncertain terms, exactly what he wanted to "do" with me;

the where, the how-big, the how-many-times were all laid out, directly from his Blackberry to my email. It was surprising behavior, but it sounded like an adventure: another clinical trial for the science project.

I picked him up at the Standard Hotel, and we went to the Chateau Marmont for drinks. Suddenly the sweet, gentle guy I met in Jackson Hole—or was it the jerk who left me stinky in Seattle?—was all over me. He backed me up against the elevator wall and was exceedingly touchy-feely on the couch at the Marmont bar.

The evening before, he had been schmoozing with the Hollywood elite, soliciting support for an international humanitarian organization. Now he was telling me about the female parking valet at his hotel who sold him pot and whom, by the way, he wanted to bend over a chair and fuck. What a one-eighty. It was all so unprofessional. It made me feel very uncomfortable, so I told him so.

> "Scott, I don't think it's cool for you to behave this way. You represent people who are doing important work."

He remained silent for a moment, then changed the subject right back to sex. He was determined, and I was getting slightly tipsy. With all his talk, by the time we finished our drinks, I was pretty worked up.

When we left the Chateau Marmont, the rain was coming down hard. As we stood waiting at the valet stand alongside a Hollywood starlet and tabloid regular, I had a flashback to the night in Seattle. Would he behave that way again? I tried to reassure myself. If nothing else, I was his ride to the airport that night; he couldn't just leave and walk miles in the rain to LAX. Well, even if he did, I was curious about what would happen next.

After fighting traffic, we made it back to my house with time to spare, having taken all available shortcuts and back roads. Soon after we walked into my house, he started kissing me and putting his hands up my shirt. With his impending flight, we were on a schedule.

He had gained weight since our last encounter; I slid my hand down his body and discovered a hefty jellyroll around his middle, a major surprise. For all his big talk, the whole thing lasted only a few minutes. It was the worst sex I have ever had. I can still hear the sound of my jeans and studded belt hitting the bamboo floor; he practically came before they landed. Granted, he had to get to the airport, but I definitely expected more. I guess some things never change.

As I drove him to the airport, I realized how selfish he was, a real sexual predator. In a repeat of history, I once again felt hurt and used. It was the same feeling I had in Seattle, but at least this time he didn't leave me smelling of stinky, old, dirty socks.

For better or worse, we still email occasionally. Just recently, I needed a business contact and knew he would be a good source. He gave me the information I needed without question.

While I do not respect his personal behavior, I respect the work he does and can keep that channel open. Taking the high road to keep things professional has given me confidence in the woman I am and what I stand for. I think he realizes this, no matter how important his title, how many influential people he rubs elbows with or how badly he behaves. He will return that call or answer that business question as our paths continue to cross.

My experience with Scott stays very front-burner in my life; the organization he works with gets a lot of daily press, not only because of the important global work they are doing but because of the level of the celebrities involved. But for every day, I am reminded of him and his over-hyped sexual abilities. I am also reminded that I am strong, and grateful that I do not burn my bridges.

Chapter Thirteen

JAMES
How Honest Is Too Honest?

February 2005

JAMES IS AN old friend I've known since junior high school. Along with Julie, whom I've known since kindergarten, and Matt, our high school friend, we have a lot of shared history. James was best man at Julie and Matt's wedding; over the years, James and I have seen each other at countless parties. Whenever we've run into one another in the past, I've always been involved with someone else. Even though I have always thought he is strikingly good looking, smart and funny, it never occurred to me that we could be more than friends. We're like a pair of old jeans: comfortable and broken in.

James and I reconnected recently at an old friend's fortieth birthday party. It was the first time I had seen him in about a year, and this time I did not have a boyfriend. The disco-themed party had an excellent band playing all the hits of the era, an open bar and a hundred or so people getting their groove on in hilarious yet hideous seventies garb. Most everyone at the party knew each other from our teenage years. It had all the ingredients for a great night—one that would go down in history.

Between the two of us, James and I hit the open bar a few too many times. After the party, Julie and Matt insisted we stay at their house. We spent the night cuddling on their couch; it was gentle and sweet. There was a comfortable connection that only occurs between two people who know one another so well.

A week later, James and I double dated with Julie and Matt. I had heard from Julie that James was excited to see me; I was excited to see him as well. When I walked into the restaurant, I was a little nervous, but in a good, schoolgirl crush kind of way.

There he stood at five-foot-seven, with his olive skin, dark hair and eyes, looking as handsome as ever. He was very kissable; his jeans and jacket were a far cry from the polyester shirt, bellbottoms and terrible hat he'd worn at the party. Over drinks and dinner, the four of us had a great time playing catch up and reminiscing.

After dinner, James and I went to a local Irish pub for a nightcap. It was so nice to be able to start conversation in the middle, without all of that "Where are you from?" and "What do you do?" banter, the dreaded "first date interview." I already knew that James is an English literature teacher at a private high school, and that he loves to surf. He already knew that I am a native Angelino who loves to snowboard. We just talked about life.

After drinks, he invited me back to his apartment. As I followed him in my own car, I was nervous and excited. We had always hung out with groups of friends, but this was going to be the first time on our own. It felt different and right.

We sat on his couch, listening to music and reading from a book as he prepared for his English lit class. He read passages aloud to me; it all felt very adult and intellectual. Without trying to be romantic, he was. He handed me the esoteric book to read with him. We both read passages aloud and laughed, agreeing that it sounded like gibberish.

Somewhere in between laughs, we started kissing. He smelled good, which, given my acute sense of smell, is a crucial factor (my ex-boyfriend used to say I could work at the airport with the dogs sniffing out drugs and explosives). James was the perfect gentleman on every level.

We lay on his couch kissing for hours. Delicate and calm, everything flowed naturally. Around 2:00 am, he asked me if I wanted to spend the night; I accepted his invitation. He held my hand, walking me into his bedroom. Without turning on the light, we kissed some more in his bed, got under the covers, and fell asleep spooning. All very innocent; the evening was flawless.

In the morning when I woke up, I noticed the numerous surfboards hanging on the wall over his bed, reflecting his passion for surfing. Watching him sleep, I appreciated the tranquility of the moment, taking note of the details that attracted me to him: the tattoo on his inner arm, his hairless, well-toned body against mine. He looked very sexy and smelled so good. When he awoke, we talked more about life as we lay there holding hands. Then he asked me: "When is the last time you had sex?"

> Without thinking, I told him the truth. "Just a few days ago."

At that time, I was casually seeing two men, Dave the Sweater Guy, and Kevin. It flew out of my mouth before I even thought about it. But everything was so comfortable; to lie or edit myself would have been out of the question. I had no choice but be honest. From James, there was dead silence. Then he changed the subject.

High school was long ago, but hey, girls will be girls. Later in the day, I got a call from Julie, asking how the night went. I told her all the juicy details: how much I enjoyed spending time with him, how I hadn't thought about Kevin at all. Normally, Kevin would have crept into my thoughts on some level or another, but with James, I did not think about him. I told Julie that I might have divulged a bit of information I should not have.

She said that her husband spoke with James that morning, and he'd said I was very honest, reassuring me it was major compliment coming from James. Based on his past with dishonest women, he respected me for being upfront. But I wondered—was I too honest? I did some bar research (asking guys in bars for their opinions) on the topic and came to the conclusion that I was. So much for the old cliché "honesty is the best policy."

Since that night we have exchanged emails and played phone tag; we talk about getting together. He presented me with a caveat about the current state of his emotional well-being: "I feel like seeing people is like inviting them out onto a lake of thin ice." I let him know that I am a really good skater, but that first and foremost I am his friend. No pressure.

Julie and I had dinner soon after my date with James, and I got an earful. She is convinced we are going to be together, and she may be right. James was celebrating his birthday with a few other guys at another restaurant, and I insisted we walk over there, even though it was "boys' night out." Her husband had asked that we not stop by, so I took full responsibility for crashing their party.

When we got to their table, I leaned in to take James' hand and wish him a happy birthday. There was an engaging sparkle in his eye and that comfortable feeling was back, with a little schoolgirl crush thrown in for good measure.

Who knows what the future has planned for us; maybe we will be together one day. I am leaving it to fate. James is a good man, and has been very honest with me about what he wants. Goodness knows, I was honest with him—maybe too honest, but at least he knows he can trust me to tell the truth.

My straightforwardness may have changed the direction of our relationship; the jury is still out on that. But in the meantime, I cherish our history and take great confidence in our friendship. There's an old saying: "Don't ask the question if you don't want to hear the answer." But another one goes, "You can have too much of a good thing." Maybe in this situation, there was just too much honesty.

Chapter Fourteen

DAMON
"Hey, Shorty!"

March 2005

BACK IN JANUARY, I had planned a spring trip to Colorado, and I was looking forward spending time in the Rockies. Between Dave, Kevin and James, the trip would also give me breathing space from the science project. Steamboat Springs is one of my favorite mountain towns, one I have spent a lot of time in, so I planned a trip. Something about Steamboat reminds me of the Old West; it's a small ranch town with a laid-back vibe that's different from most mountain resorts and ski areas. As I landed in the tiny Hayden airport, it felt like I was coming home.

After picking up my gear from baggage claim, I boarded the local shuttle van to the hotel. My only thoughts were of food, sleep and waking up early to get on the mountain.

I checked into my room, dropped off my gear and went straight to the restaurant. I was famished. I was craving a big plate of salty, fatty, Mexican food from Dos Amigos, a restaurant I've frequented on my countless trips to Steamboat. I used to go there often with a man I dated years ago.

I know the ratio of men to women in a ski town is uneven, but a girl can dream of a quiet meal on her own. With a trendy *Black Book* magazine and iPod in hand, I looked forward to a quiet meal; I had no intention of meeting or even speaking to a man, but you've heard me say that before.

When I arrived, there was only one seat left at the bar. It just happened to be next to a very handsome man in his twenties. I tried not to notice him, but as I read and listened to music, he noticed me. I must have looked extremely hungry. Was it the way I clutched the fork and knife with no food in front of me? Perhaps he noticed that the bartender seemed in no hurry to serve me. Before he even introduced himself, he offered me some of his quesadilla. I politely declined, but we immediately began talking. Damon was very tall with brown hair, big hazel eyes and a great build; he wore jeans and a t-shirt, with a heavy jacket slung over his chair. Through conversation, I learned he manages the local paint store.

We had a good time, talking about everything and nothing at the same time. He was curious about what was on my iPod, so, ever hygiene-conscious, I asked him if his ears were clean. He let me look into them and they were spotless, so I handed him my headphones. I never intended to use my iPod as a pickup tool, but there I was with a hot, friendly guy looking into his ears for wax and dirt.

He invited me back to his condo, which was within walking distance of the restaurant. I told myself I was going to be good. *Jennifer, do not pay attention to the strapping young man in front you. Put your horns and tail away.*

He offered me a beer and opened one for himself. I opted for water—I'd had enough to drink between the wine on the plane and tequila at dinner—and took a seat on his couch. He hooked my iPod up to his stereo and we listened to some of my music collection while continuing our conversation.

As we talked, he kept inching closer. I asked, "Should we just get this over with and kiss?" And we did. It was a sensual kiss, and I wanted more. I could feel his thick-gauge tongue piercing against my tongue, very sexy. I was a goner.

Maybe it was because of the alcohol in my system, but the situation was hard to resist. The horns and tail were growing. I thought to myself, *Is this the behavior of a thirty-nine-year-old woman?* Apparently so! He picked me up and carried me into his bedroom. I couldn't think of a single reason to fight it. Then my mind wandered to Kevin as Damon laid me down on his bed.

At the time, I was seeing Kevin back at home; no matter how I tried to resist him, the attraction was strong. It was all for science, of course, but I still I felt myself getting emotionally entangled. Kevin was so unavailable to me on so many levels; we were unavailable to one another. I think that was part of the draw.

Kevin and I had made no commitments to be exclusive. Damon was right there, sweet and ever so frisky. So was I at that point. I decided to forget about Kevin, focus on the science project, and be present with this young, handsome guy who was clearly into me. The feeling was mutual.

We made out for a while, listening to Flogging Molly and Social Distortion. It was very steamy. Regaining my composure after about an hour, we said good night. It was hard to leave, but it felt right. I was tired from traveling all day and wanted to be out on the mountain early. He was a gentleman, kissing me good night at his doorstep. I gave him my business card with my room number at the Sheraton written on the back, and returned to the hotel for a good night's sleep.

The next day, after an incredible time on the mountain, Damon called to make plans for the evening. We met at a restaurant located on the base of the mountain for dinner and drinks. After dinner, we went back to the Sheraton for drinks at the hotel bar. We each had one cocktail for decorum's sake and went straight to up to the room.

We had an awesome time making out, which led to even better sex. It was good fun—more, I think, than we both expected. We were comfortable with each other, and soon after fell asleep spooning. There was a very real connection between two people—more than just a one-night stand. Damon showed more maturity and attentiveness than any of the other men I'd been with during my "research." Even though he was only twenty-seven, he treated me like a woman and behaved like a real man. I almost forgot I was a "scientist."

Damon had to go to work early the next morning, reluctantly leaving around 5:00 a.m. As the alarm clock buzzed us awake, it was still dark and cold outside; we were sleepy, warm and comfortably spooning. We both wanted him to stay, but he is a responsible man, a man of character. As he got dressed, we talked about meeting that night for drinks. We kissed goodbye, making it even harder for him to leave.

I had another exceptional day out on the mountain, and I was looking forward to seeing Damon later that night after having dinner with some old friends. I took the local bus back up to the mountain area; Damon and I had made plans to meet at Slopeside. As I walked toward the restaurant, I could see his very tall silhouette. "Hey, Shorty," he called out. So endearing—he already had a nickname for me. We hugged hello, and I noticed immediately that he seemed down. I asked him what was wrong. Damon shared with me that his mom had called earlier in the day to tell him that his father's leukemia had returned.

He looked so sad. I was completely tongue-tied. It was

not what I was expecting, but you never know what life will bring. I put my arm around him, my interest in romance evaporating. I just wanted to be a friend, someone he could talk to if he felt like talking. I was happy to be there for him.

We had one drink at Slopeside, and since it was getting really smoky in the bar area, we decided to go someplace else. It seemed strange to talk about his dad's cancer while sitting there breathing in carcinogens.

We found a quieter, smoke free spot, drank beers and talked. It became very clear to me how close he is with his family, and how strong his father's resolve is. I knew exactly how it felt to watch someone you love die; my grandmother's lymphoma was hard on our entire family. Damon and I bonded on a spiritual level. I was so glad I could be there for him. He is very aware of the value of the people in his life—a trait I admire. It is always so interesting to me how life evolves, and how people come into our lives at certain times. As they say, timing is everything.

He walked me back to the Sheraton and we hung out in the room a while, talking. He appeared to be physically tired and emotionally drained. We kissed each other on the cheek and hugged good night, promising to keep in touch. We have. He still calls me "Shorty."

Damon is an extraordinary person, and I feel lucky to have met him. I was only in Steamboat Springs for three days, but we made a very real connection. We had great conversations and a unique physical connection that was more than just sex. Most importantly, we created a friendship, something real and lasting that transcends age difference, time and geography.

I'm so glad I didn't listen to the self-censor that told me I was too old for him. It would have been my loss. Damon made me realize what all the men I'd been with in the last year were missing—a real maturity, an openness that he had in spades. I want someone in my life that values people as much as I do, and he helped to remind me that it's possible.

Damon knew about the book I was writing, and on my return to LA, he submitted his version of our weekend together in case I needed it. He was the only "subject" who offered me this kind of feedback. I think that says a lot about his character and confidence.

It is amazing that out on the path, while looking for a man who is emotionally available, I found Damon. He is that specimen of man who is open to life's adventures. He's not afraid of being real, present and vulnerable. It gives me hope that there are more like him out there. The available man exists; he's just rare.

Chapter Fifteen

The Pheromone Factor

The term "pheromone" comes from the ancient Greek words "pherein": to carry, and "hormon": to excite.

—James V. Kohl, Michaela Atzmueller,
Bernhard Fink and Karl Grammer,
Human Pheromones:
Integrating Neuroendocrinology and Ethology

DURING MY YEAR of science, I put the male population under a microscope. I read a plethora of books and magazine articles, extensively researching the mysteries of attraction. Questions kept coming up in my mind: In the process of human mating, what attracts us to particular people? Why can one person love a too-short, too-hairy mate that another person would find unattractive? Is it chemistry? Is it instinct? Maybe it's pheromones.

Humans naturally produce pheromones, a chemical compound released through the sweat glands in the skin. According to Dr. Winnifred Cutler, PhD, "Pheromones are naturally occurring substances the fertile body excretes externally, conveying airborne messages that generate social responses from others of the same species."[26] In other words, pheromones are nature's way of signaling attraction on a primal, genetic level.

Some researchers believe that humans have the capability to detect pheromones subliminally through the vomeronasal organ (VNO)—two microscopic holes in the septum of the nose—just as other animals do. The VNO is well documented in rodents. Rats use it to detect pheromones in each other's urine, which helps them identify the gender of a potential mate. This sense also allows the rat to find a mate with a dissimilar immune system, which gives any offspring the ability to fight off a wider range of infections.[27]

There are four types of pheromones that serve a variety of purposes: repellants, bonding pheromones, synchronizers and attractors. Male dogs use repellant pheromones in their urine to mark their territory; bonding pheromones allow babies to recognize their mothers. The phenomenon of close-knit groups of women sharing a menstrual cycle is attributed to synchronizing pheromones. And then there is attraction: "Some pheromones serve to promote the sexual attractiveness of the wearer and elicit romantic attention from the opposite sex."[28]

Just as conscious smells can attract or repel, pheromones can trigger similar responses. In most animals, the relationship between mating and pheromones is straightforward. Pheromones allow animals to recognize like species for potential mates.

Sea urchins release pheromones into the water, triggering other sea urchins to emit their sex cells simultaneously. Gypsy moths use pheromones to overcome great distances when mating. The female gypsy moth releases her unique pheromone through her abdomen and flaps her wings, dispersing it into the air. Since female gypsy moths don't fly, they wait in trees for their signals to be received; they are rarely disappointed. Males can detect a female from great distances, even up to seven miles away. The moth pheromone is so powerful that one female can attract more than a billion males.[29] If only it were that easy for us. Imagine perching on a branch with a billion men vying for your attention.

However, we as humans are more complex. Scientists are divided as to whether we react to pheromones the way other animals do. The research into human reaction to pheromones is ongoing as science tries to determine just how human pheromones work. Because humans are highly individualized, the pheromones we produce are equally diverse and not always detectable. Add that to our tendency to "over shower" (it's possible that even one shower a day is too much), covering up our own natural pheromones with cologne, perfume and deodorants. With all that spritzing and spraying, we could be missing out on a potential mate by hiding behind synthetic scents—or you could get a reaction like Pepe Le Pew.

The debate surrounding pheromones—their effectiveness, their benefits, even their existence in humans—is ongoing. It is interesting to note that studies by Dr. Cutler in the 1970s "showed that women who have regular sex with men have more regular menstrual cycles than woman who have sporadic sex. Regular sex delayed the decline of estrogen and made women more fertile. This led the research team to look for what the man was providing in the equation. By 1986, they realized it was the pheromones."[30]

Those kinds of revelations got my mind running in overdrive. In my own life experiences, I have certainly been aware of the power of scent, but the idea of seemingly undetectable essences guiding our attractions and connections was very intriguing. The more I learned about pheromones, the more fascinated I became.

Still in scientist mode, I decided to do a little research of my own. I discovered that numerous Internet businesses sell little bottles of human pheromones for between fifty and one hundred dollars: attraction in a bottle. I was unclear as to how to determine the real from the fake, the snake oil from the real thing. Maybe it's all a scam. Playing on the basic human desire to connect, both brands I purchased promised special secret ingredients for "extra attraction." One claimed to contain an Egyptian ingredient, added to the human pheromones androstenol and copulins, for a total of "3 genuine effective human pheromones." There is such a veil of secrecy around the contents of these products; I hoped I wasn't unknowingly giving my fellow scientists camel dung extract or donkey ball essence to wear like perfume.

The claims seemed a little far-fetched. I felt like I was being seduced by a scam equivalent to buying Dr. Stanley's Liniment from a traveling salesman back in the 1800s. Life is a biological masterpiece and I find everything about the way we function to be a true miracle. To have the ability to extract and put up for sale something that can bring love and attraction, help you to close a business deal, or make more friends as you walk down the street really goes against my beliefs. Despite my skepticism, I ordered some. While I waited patiently (but excitedly) for love-in-a-bottle to arrive via U.S. mail, I assembled my eager test subjects.

For the first group test, I recruited three of my beautiful, inspired friends to hit the bar scene wearing the Internet-purchased pheromones.

It was a summer Friday night in Santa Monica, clear and warm. When each of my friends arrived at the restaurant, I asked them to put a tiny drop from bottle #1 behind their ears. The directions state that the pheromone is so potent, you should "use only a single drop." Too much could have the reverse effect. Since the directions also claim the contents are "the most powerful love potion in the world," I wanted to be sure we all followed the directions to the letter.

Pheromones sparingly applied, we ate dinner, drank wine and excitedly waited for something to happen. After an hour or so, the only man who approached us needed to borrow the extra chair from our table.

Getting a little frustrated at the lack of results, I asked the bus boy what he thought of the women at the table. He didn't say a word; in fact, he looked a little confused and intimidated. There was a lot of boobage going on and we looked hot. The question was, were we hot because of our sexy outfits, or was there some kind of deeper animal thing going on? Could he sense the pheromones?

He never came back to the table, but I was convinced that he felt the animalistic heat emanating from our pack and was too nervous to return. Of course, he may have just been busy with other tables.

After dinner, my beautiful friends and I walked two blocks to a major Santa Monica pickup place, where we surveyed the bar. The women-to-men ratio was out of balance, and definitely not in our favor. But armed with our pheromones, we were confident that we would stand out like a pack in heat. Men of the club scene, be forewarned!

We all got drinks and stood around in the noisy, crowded club, shouting our attempts at girl-chat. Nothing seemed to be happening. Where was the call of the wild? Why were we not surrounded by packs of men?

Collectively, we began to notice the pungent and overwhelming scent of perfume in the air. Maybe the chemical smells were overpowering our animal essences. Oh, the irony! The noise could have also been a factor. The pounding bass of the sound system was almost deafening, making it difficult to strike up a conversation. I worried my research was in danger of being a bust until a group of very tall and handsome men walked in, accompanied by an overly made up and coiffed blonde woman who seemed a little insecure. When I approached them, she gave me a defensive look.

As I walked up, I detected a foreign accent and asked them where they were from. According to the most outgoing and most handsome of the bunch, they were from the Czech Republic and had been in the U.S. only three days. I welcomed them to California and reported back to my friends. Our beautiful, blonde, alpha-friend moved in on the dark-haired guy with model good looks.

The two of them talked while the rest of us chatted amongst ourselves. A few minutes later, she came back to give us more details: They were all professional hockey players and have been in the States for three years. *What?* He just told me three days. In a bold move, testing the power of the little blue bottle (it said "guaranteed" after all), I called him on this misinformation. I walked up and asked him point-blank why he lied.

He looked taken aback, paused for a split second and said to me, "You are not as smart as you think." I was in a state of shock. No one had ever called me stupid—at least not to my face. I suddenly realized how people could get into bar fights. I wanted to punch the guy's lights out or kick him in the crotch. But I remained ladylike.

I have never in my entire life had a man say something so utterly rude to me. The movie in my mind played out a little something like this: "Oh, you are so right. I am really very dumb. You must be brilliant, being a handsome, European hockey player. My friend, who you are trying to pick up, will surely love the fact that you just insulted me. I bet she really wants to go home to have wild and passionate sex with you now. And you are questioning *my* intelligence?"

In reality, I said nothing and walked away. He was not worth any more of my time. Then it occurred to me that this moment could have been brought on by the pheromones in the little blue bottle. Perhaps it brought out the caveman aggressiveness. Or maybe he was just hands down the rudest and most arrogant person I had ever met. While I would never know for sure, I felt further research into this phenomenon would be necessary.

When I woke up the next morning, I was excited to continue with the experiment as planned. Via email, I enlisted six more women to participate in the science project fun. One of my deductions was that loud and smelly places make it difficult to test the pheromones. I thought it best to get a broad sample of women who could try two different formulas in their everyday lives. My instructions to all the women were to apply it, go about daily life and see what happens.

Given the "secret" nature of the formulas, I was not quite sure what I was handing out. I hoped it was more than just castor oil in those opaque, colored bottles. Vial #1, the blue bottle, was filled with androstenol, copulins and other secret ingredients; the word "guaranteed" was printed boldly in black on the silver label. Vial # 2, the brown bottle, contained the special "Egyptian" formula with a pharaoh-like image printed on the label. Each woman was asked to wear the colorless, odorless oil from vial #1 for a week, then switch to vial #2 for another week, and report to me their findings. A week later, I purchased a third vial and sent it out to a smaller sample of women for more testing.

The nine women I chose were from diverse backgrounds and of varying ages, ethnicities and relationship histories. All were enthusiastic about the project: my willing guinea pigs on the prowl.

The Pheromone Test

I sent the test subjects out with their instructions while I continued to do my own testing. Wearing the vial #2 "Egyptian" pheromone, I went to have dinner in San Diego with two of my fellow scientists, Snowflake Alcaraz and Danika, and their respective partners Dan and Barry. The two couples had never met, and I'd never met Dan. There seemed to be something to the aggression thing after all. Just as the

Czech man became aggressive in our presence, there was a tension between the two men at our table, and Danika's husband got very upset during dinner. Dan and Barry are like apples and oranges. Dan is boisterous with a sharp wit; Barry, a stem cell research scientist, is much more serious and reserved.

Barry seemed very uncomfortable with the banter at the table. As the dinner wore on, Danika became increasingly quiet; I sensed she was well beyond her comfort level. It was not long before Barry said they had to leave, something about waking up early for a bike ride with his boss. It got even uglier when Dan made a comment about Barry's excuse for their early departure.

Needless to say, I felt incredibly bad about the whole situation. Dan and I got along well—I understood his wit—but the next day, when I spoke with Danika, I learned that Barry felt Dan was being rude. I wondered if the pheromones caused the tension between the two men. Danika and I agreed that something was different about Barry. He had been under a lot stress at work, so it could have been that—or maybe it was the combination of it all.

I came to the conclusion that the Egyptian formula, the same stuff I marked "vial # 2" for my research subjects, was quite a volatile substance. I was anxious to hear about the experiences from my group of science lovers, and when their results came in, they were truly fascinating.

Stella
Age: 38
Height: 5' 7"
Weight: 150 lbs.
Occupation: Realtor
Relationship Status: Single

Vial # 1—Stella found a lingering effect from vial #1. She applied one day, forgot to apply the next, and came back with similar results both days: more attention from men and women. Two significant events followed. The first was a second date with "Owen." The first had been enjoyable and ended with kissing. On the second date, "there was a lot of attraction and kissing right off the bat." A terrific date and passionate evening ensued. Stella reports feeling "stunned that we had such a fantastic time together. It blew my mind."

The second noteworthy event began the next night. Stella was working late with a male co-worker, after which they went out for a beer. A beer turned into a walk on the beach, which turned into sitting and kissing in the sand. "Then he went down on me, and I on him, and it was all good."

> Note from Stella: *Before Thursday night, I had not had sex in one and a half years, so this was a huge amount of sexual activity for me. Also, I'm usually a one-man woman, so two different men in two days is unusual for me.*

Vial #2—Stella met up once again with Owen, "and it was crazy." She reports that the date went much the same as the last.

●●●

Snowflake Alcaraz
Age: 48
Height: 5' 6"
Weight: 160 lbs.
Occupation: College Professor, Writer/Editor
Relationship Status: Long-term Relationship (13 years)

Vial #1—On Snowflake Alcaraz's first evening out, she attended a party where a man she knew not to be "touchy put his arm around me. Very uncharacteristic." During the course of the evening, more people touched her as they leaned in to speak, and gave her considerably more compliments than usual. She also mentioned the club was very warm, perhaps intensifying the potency of the pheromone.

The next day Snowflake had to be fingerprinted for her teaching job. The two police officers "at the window play-fought over who would get to print me." The winning officer took her through the process, which involved a good bit of hand touching. After several tries, the particularly chatty officer informed Snowflake that he wasn't getting good prints and asked if he could wipe her hands with an aloe lotion to activate the printing. She agreed. "It was like a trip to the spa."

That evening, Snowflake joined a former student and his wife—whom she'd never met—for happy hour. "I was sure to sit right next to wifey, because the vials do indeed seem to have some sort of power." Snowflake and the woman got along great, almost excluding the male at the table. "She touched my arm near hers, laughed a lot, and was pretty complimentary." Snowflake reports that the woman wasn't flirting, but she was friendly.

Starting work at a new school, Snowflake reported that

"it's either the friendliest place in the world to work, or vial #1 is doing its job." She was unsure of the effect on her boyfriend Dan's libido, but "he's a little less likely to accept a brush-off when I have it on."

Overall, vial #1 appeared to have positive reactions in both genders, "with people being friendly and open with me overall," but particularly on women. "They seem more drawn to me when I have it on."

Vial #2—Reports are incomplete, but it seems to be making "Dan nuts because he's been chasing me relentlessly since I got home."

Vial # 3—Snowflake reported that the third formula "works more on the lads again. My male students chose to sit very close, chat me up more, buy me a coffee, etc." The reactions did not seem to be sexually or romantically motivated, but men were very friendly. "It seems to create a very approachable scent."

●●●

Sophie
Age: 48
Height: 5' 7"
Weight: 130 lbs.
Occupation: Group Exercise Manager/Instructor
Relationship Status: Widowed

Vial # 1—Sophie reported that during the first couple of days, she received pleasant comments from "unexpected sources." As the week wore on, though, she was aware of men being more attentive to her, as well as more complimentary. The most substantial effect Sophie noted was during the spinning class she teaches. "Men seem to be gravitating toward the front row," she reports, while both men and women "seem to be going out of their way to greet and compliment me."

Vial # 2—Sophie immediately noticed an increase in the number of men that approached her, "both at work and in public," to the point that her daughter also noticed the extra attention. It even brought out good behavior in her surly brother-in-law.

•••

Danika
Age: 29
Height: 5' 7"
Weight: 130 lbs.
Occupation: Teacher
Relationship Status: Married

Vial # 1—Danika noticed nothing out of the ordinary during the first week of testing—not even with her husband. However, she did report that one of her less motivated students "surprisingly volunteered to stay after school on a Friday for tutoring and to retake a test."

Vial # 2—Danika did not see much of a difference with vial # 2, although "I only used it for three days but during that time our sex life was better and has been better ever since." But Danika's husband was adversely affected when they went out to dinner with three women wearing the # 2 pheromone. "He was acting so different when we all had the pheromones on at the table. I have never seen my husband like that."

•••

Taylor
Age: 24
Height: 5' 9"
Weight: 140 lbs.
Job: Receptionist
Relationship Status: Single, Never Married

Vial # 1—"Attracts men and women to me. It's all good!"

Vial #2—"Men and women are not so nice when [I'm] wearing #2."

•••

Georgia
Age: 37
Height: 5' 9½"
Weight: 140 lbs.
Occupation: Yoga Instructor
Relationship Status: Single, Never Married

Vial # 1—Georgia noticed no change in people's reactions while wearing # 1.

Vial # 2—Georgia felt there were too many variables to allow for a conclusive report, but noticed a bit more attention wearing # 2.

•••

Giselle
Age: 35
Height: 5'10"
Weight: 145 lbs.
Occupation: Business Owner/Marketing Advertising Consultant
Relationship Status: Single, Never Married

Vial # 2—On her first outing, Giselle wore the formula from vial # 2 and noted nothing unusual. Going about her day-to-day, she found that overall nothing changed: "The same amount of strangers are friendly, and the same amount of men who flirt, still flirt." She did, however, notice odd behavior from the manager at a restaurant she has frequented for years. In the past, he has always been friendly, but "when I went there wearing #2, he literally couldn't keep away. He constantly came around and always touched the back of my chair, even when he walked by without stopping." This occurrence was marked by the presence of another test subject, Magdalena. Giselle speculates that the combination of the two pheromone-laden women brought out the strange behavior. In all other instances, vial #2 seemed to have no effect on people's reaction to Giselle.

Vial # 1—Giselle went out two weekend nights in a row and again experienced no changes in the behavior in the people around her.

●●●

Lily
Age: 24
Height: 5' 2"
Weight: 140 lbs.
Occupation: Retail Mail Clerk
Relationship Status: Long-term Relationship

Vial # 2—Lily also began with vial # 2. She immediately noticed a change in her boyfriend, Mark. On their weekly Friday night dinner-and-a-movie date, he was very agitated and distant at dinner. "I asked what was wrong and he said nothing, so I tried to ignore it." Back at his place, he was still acting oddly, so she asked him to take her home. After she was home for about thirty minutes, Mark called to apologize "for being out of it."

The next day, Lily forgot to put on the formula before she and her boyfriend went on a picnic with her family. Everything seemed back to normal. After lunch, she "remembered to put on the formula, and again, after about ten or fifteen minutes of being around Mark, he started acting as though he didn't want me around." But his behavior was only hostile to her—he was relaxed and polite with her family.

In general, Lily noticed that aside from her boyfriend's unusual behavior, she got more looks from men at the gym and at work. Her co-workers became more helpful and considerate—one co-worker with whom relations are generally tense and uncomfortable even acted more polite and friendly. "We actually joked for a whole two or three minutes on subjects unrelated to work."

Vial # 1—On the first day of vial # 1, Lily and her co-worker were back to their "not speaking terms," but she and her boyfriend were back to being happy together.

●●●

Magdalena
Age: 51
Height: 5' 9"
Weight: 139 lbs.
Occupation: Sales Director for a softwear company
Relationship Status: Divorced

Vial # 1—Magdalena noticed an overall increase in attention paid to her, including the older man who regularly stands in front of her in yoga class. One noteworthy encounter was with an eighteen-month-old baby girl in a restaurant "who was relentless in her pursuit of my attention, including talking on my cell phone and blowing me kisses." Animals also paid particular attention to Magdalena; other people's pets, as well as her two cats, could not stay away.

Vial # 2—"I believe #1 is the cat's meow, but not #2."

•••

Jennifer Kelton
Age: 39
Height: 5' 4"
Weight: 125 lbs.
Occupation: Writer
Relationship status: Single, Never Married

Vial #1—I have had fun with it. Men are more touchy-feely and buy me drinks at the bar much more frequently; the men who know me seem to be constantly rubbing up against me. Can we say dog in heat?! I am still testing #1 and have ordered a second bottle. For me this was the most powerful.

Vial #2—It seems to bring out more aggressive behavior in both men and women, and not in a good way. I would never put on #2 again. I am a very friendly person and the repellant factor was unmistakable. Maybe there is camel dung in that little brown bottle. For me the whole vial # 2 experience was uncomfortable.

Vial #3—The first time I wore it men were all over me, even giving me back rubs at the bar. I also got a long checkout by a famous actor at the gym. After that, the reaction was friendly, but not over the top. I am not convinced that #3 really did anything. The funny thing is that this brand cost the most and had the most hype on the website.

•••

The Placebo Test

All good scientists know you need a control group, so after two weeks of experimentation, I sent out two of my subjects with a placebo. I gave Lily and Stella each two bottles: one yellow, one blue. They did not know which bottle contained the "real" stuff and which I filled with plain jojoba oil.

Lily

It was hard for me not to spill the beans to Lily. Through business, we see each other almost daily. About a week in, I asked her what she thought, and she was sure she'd figured out which was which. It was hard for me to keep a poker face as she told me how she had figured it out.

> When I used blue, I got more attention than with yellow; the days I had on yellow were like any other day. With blue, my coworkers are nicer, more respectful and did me little favors; and my boyfriend is more interested. I can totally tell the difference between the two.

> It is also so important to bring up that fact that one of my coworkers and I are like oil and water. But when I had on blue, we joked around with each other. That's when I was like, "Wha-ho, this really works!" He actually offered to help me with a project I was working on outside of the workplace. He took fifteen to twenty minutes of his own time. When I had yellow on, he was back to his old hostile, mean self.

When I finally revealed that she was right, she replied, "I knew it! It was so obvious!"

Stella

What I love most about Stella is the way she will throw caution to the wind. Every time we go out, she really lets loose, and the night I gave her the placebo pheromones was no different. We met at the Baja Cantina for drinks after her yoga class, and she walked in with wet hair, looking relaxed. I gave her the two vials—the yellow placebo and the blue pheromones. Without knowing which was which, she put on the potion from the blue bottle.

Before she arrived, I struck up a conversation with the two men sitting next to me. They were not my type at all, but they seemed nice—until one of them reached over into my tortilla chip basket and took a handful. Baja Cantina offers free chips, self-serve style; you could eat them all night long and no one would care or even notice. But the fact that he did not bother to get his own seemed weird to me and for him to just reach over into my food crossed a huge boundary. I told him to "get his hands out of my basket," and he became "Mr. Basket" from there.

When Stella arrived, we shared a quesadilla while she

and Mr. Basket became engaged in conversation. When we finished eating, the two men asked us to go out on the patio for more drinks and conversation. Mr. Basket was clearly into Stella.

As we sat outside, I began to talk to the two Englishmen at the table next to us, and joined them when Mr. Basket's friend lit a cigarette. A few minutes passed, and when I turned around to check on Stella, I saw her kissing Mr. Basket. Those same boundary-crossing hands that reached for my chips were now on my friend. Shortly after, they left the bar together. The blue vial was in full effect!

We checked in the next morning via telephone and Stella told me that while they had sex, she was not sure if the blue vial worked. She planned to alternate daily with the yellow bottle and after a week, gave me her verdict.

> I feel more of a reaction with the yellow. Even driving on the road, when I have yellow on men will say hi, and women are more friendly.
>
> It was hard to tell this week because I was getting my period, and I was stressed at work. I am not sure if the pheromones affect your hormones. I put blue on and, at that time, I was experiencing premenstrual angst, notable because my senses seemed heightened. I wondered, *Is my body being confused by the pheromones?*
>
> Coming into the office this week, I managed to keep my pants on, but co-workers were drawn to me. I was asked to host an open house at a 3.8 million dollar property.

> Still, with the blue I am very emotional. I'm not sure what is going on. Yellow seems stronger and more potent; it makes me feel different. I send out vibes and people get it.

After Stella gave me her report, I revealed that in fact the blue bottle contained the real pheromones. We both laughed and talked about the findings: the placebo results were split, 50-50.

The Conclusion

After testing three different brands of pheromones and a placebo, people who knew what I was up to all asked the same question: "Do they work?" That of course is the million dollar question. Can love and attraction be purchased from the Internet? Of the eleven test subjects, I may have been the most skeptical; though as Georgia pointed out, there are many variables that contribute to attraction. I would have to conclude that those little bottles of oil did seem to have an effect on people's behavior.

Perhaps some of the test subjects acted differently knowing they were wearing pheromones. Others may have been able to "forget" and act normally. The sights, smells and sounds we encounter in our daily lives could have an impact on the effectiveness, or maybe none at all. I think it really comes down to DNA, genetics and evolution. No matter how much we have evolved over millions of years, we still hold our basic mating instincts regardless of all the variables. Our intuition and our subtle, inborn instincts are still in full effect, which proves to me it is best to use what Mother Nature gave you when interfacing with life.

Chapter Sixteen

Man Test

Sometimes I wonder if men and women really suit each other. Perhaps they should live next door and just visit now and then.

—Katherine Hepburn

I CONFESS THE idea to test the pheromones on men was a complete afterthought, but in the name of amateur science, I felt it was important. Using the same plan but a different gender, I went back to the pheromone drawing board, assembling a sample group of four men, aged thirty-seven to forty-two, all of whom are single.

To keep continuity in the testing procedure, I utilized the same online company and pheromone brand used in the women's test, this time purchasing a blend created specifically for men. Interestingly, the website's advertisement describing the pheromone blend called it "the boss." *Hmmm,* I had to wonder, *the boss of whom?* It also said this particular pheromone was "featured by a recent *Dateline* special as the most potent pheromone product on the market."

When I distributed the vials, the very first thing I was asked by all four men was, "Will I get laid?" I was actually hopeful they would, as it would make for good science project fodder. Once again feeling like a drug dealer, I gave each man three little brown glass bottles: a vial marked #1, containing the real pheromones, and two more vials for the placebo test, marked A and B. Vial A had the placebo and vial B, the real pheromones. I gave the men very specific directions as to how to conduct their tests over the two-week period and told them to report the findings to me.

Dealing with two of the participants was somewhat exasperating; my other two eager recruits rocked it. I am not man bashing here, but unlike the women, who all remained present and available, two of the men proved to be finicky and difficult to work with, not responding with any kind of information or follow up. Their irresponsibility was frustrating. Was there some kind of deeper animal thing going on here? Did the hope of "getting laid" affect the man test? Maybe their spirit of science got stuck in their pants.

Male Pheromone Test Results
Ruben
Age: 39
Height: 5' 9"
Weight: 145 lbs.
Occupation: Musician/Real Estate Agent
Relationship Status: Single

Ruben was great to work with and had interesting results.

Vial #1—While perhaps he didn't make the connection at first, the pheromones did seem to have an effect on him—maybe just not the one he wanted. Ruben reported that while wearing the pheromone from vial #1, there was "no real difference. But the first night I wore it, the girl [I am dating] and I had a huge fight. She got so drunk and was pawing on every guy in sight, and then she tried to have a three-way with me and one of my very conservative and happily married friends. Pretty much a disaster. Then she passed out and remembers nothing." He added that a couple of days later, she "gave me a smoking blowjob and she is not normally all that sexual."

Ruben met a lot of girls while wearing the pheromones,

especially foreign women; however, he was not sure of the cause. "It seems like even more women of all ethnic groups are checking me out—it just seems like more activity." He also was delighted that a "way hot chick" at yoga put her mat much closer to his than needed, and "there was this total energy. She was smiling at me a lot, and she was young, early twenties, and hot."

Vials A (placebo) and B (pheromone)—My test subjects knew that one of the two vials marked A and B was a placebo, just not which one. Ruben was still puzzled about the effectiveness of the pheromones. After using both from this sample, he reported that they "had no effect on my world at all! What the…? Maybe it is not working for me. Although…Come to think of it…today I did get hit on by a very attractive Latin woman with lots of makeup." When we talked live, he told me that he thought A might be the real pheromone, "but it is so hard to tell."

We talked about his upcoming date with the very attractive Latin woman. I asked him if he would be willing to wear the pheromones around her and see what happens. After all, he had it on when they first met, and she later tracked him down at his band's gig. Unfortunately for science, she blew off the date. As for Ruben, in my opinion, it was her loss.

●●●

Chivers
Age: 42
Height: 5' 6"
Weight: 138 lbs.
Occupation: Music Executive
Relationship status: Single

Chivers was also an enthusiastic participant. When we first spoke on the phone after he began the test, I could tell he was a new man. He said very matter-of-factly, "The test has put me in a new light. My confidence is up."

Vial #1—Chivers noticed a difference in the response of women immediately. "The very first day, at Starbucks, I met a really, really, really nice girl. She was drawn to me. I was thinking, *This pheromone stuff must be working.*"

He also experienced a friendlier, outgoing vibe from friends and strangers of both genders, whenever he went out. "Both men and women were very chatty. There was this one woman that would not let me go." It continued while taking a friend from England around LA: "Doing the Hollywood thing, there was a waitress at the Skybar who smiled and talked to me. She was really cute and normally the staff there is not that friendly. I told my friend about the pheromone test, but he did not think it could work."

But it continued to work. A checker at Chivers' local supermarket, who in ten years had never commented on his appearance, complimented his hair. In the player's lounge after a tennis match, a top-ranked female player approached him, engaging him in conversation, though she had never spoken with him before. While wearing the pheromones people, especially women, were taking notice. "Every girl seemed to look at me in a different way."

Vial A (placebo) and B (pheromone)—Wearing vial A, Chivers returned to Starbucks to see if the woman there was still into him. She was. Later that day, however, at a tennis match, another top-ranked woman player he'd encountered before paid no attention. With vial B, he "felt nothing additional" but found himself being hit on by an attractive woman while out with friends at a trendy upscale nightspot. "It was hard to tell, but the big difference between A and B could have been my confidence. In the end, I really noticed a difference."

Chivers was so enthusiastic about the pheromone test results, I asked him if he wanted the link to the pheromone company. He responded, "Yes, I would like to have my own supply." Women of the world, be warned!

●●●

Holmes
Age: 37
Height: 5' 8"
Weight: 185 lbs.
Occupation: Film
Relationship Status: Single

When I gave the three vials to Holmes, I was dating him causally (see the Crab Man story in Chapter Twenty-One). I thought it would be fun to turn the tables on myself to see if I would notice when he was wearing the pheromones. He was up to the test, but we never got that far.

His first report was via email: "I have tried the first bottle and I seem to be having an allergic reaction. My skin is fine, but I am constantly sneezing—like this-stuff-is-made-out-of-cat-dander kind of sneezing. I took a break to see if it was the weather or the stuff, but I seem very sensitive to it. That was the only reaction that I have sensed so far."

Even though he was uncomfortable, he agreed to test the other two vials (either in the name of science or just to get me in bed again). Later that week I checked in to see how he was doing. He had been wearing vial B and was "fine." Funny. The B vial contained the real pheromones, and there was no allergic reaction this time.

My impression is that he is somewhat out of touch. He said how "sensitive" he was to vial #1 when he knew it was real pheromones, but when he thought he had on the fake stuff, which in fact was the real stuff, he had no adverse physical reactions. Psychosomatic reaction to the hilt! After spending a little more time with Holmes, I realized he is an extreme A-type personality, a know-it-all and a control freak.

What I have noticed, with both males and females, is the more A-type the person, the less the pheromones seem to work. Maybe the person is just so caught up in their own world that they do not perceive anything outside of what they can see and control.

The very last time I saw Holmes, I was not sure if he had the pheromones on or not, but I absolutely detested being in his company. I found it hard to even look at him and was filled with revulsion. On a dinner date at a trendy Sunset Strip restaurant I told him, "I think this is very uncomfortable and maybe you should leave." He did.

●●●

Jimmy Stingray
Age: 45
Height: 6' 0"
Weight: 200 lbs.
Occupation: Event Producer/Stage Manager
Relationship Status: Hopelessly Single

After I sent Jimmy Stingray the three vials with his instructions, I received an email stating that he would love to participate in the test, but he was unable: "I didn't realize androstenone (which the pheromone contains) is a steroid. I am very allergic to some steroids." He offered to return the vials so I could recruit a replacement.

This information brought up concerns about my other test subjects. There was no mention of possible allergic reactions on the website, so I contacted the pheromone company to confirm that androstenone is in fact a steroid. This was their reply: "In the strict scientific sense of the word, yes, androstenone is a steroid, but in the normal use of the word as a wt. [weight] lifter, 'anabolic steroid,' no it is not. Cholesterol (as found in eggs and milk) is also classified as a steroid, but as you can guess not a body building supplement." I responded that they might want to issue a warning with the product.

A couple of weeks passed, but I still hadn't heard from Jimmy Stingray. He never responded to my numerous emails inquiring about androstenone. He never got back to me. As far as I know, he still has the vials. The man at the pheromone company never responded to my suggestion about a warning label, either.

●●●

Conclusion

After looking at the man test results, it was apparent that the mind could be very powerful. It was particularly evident with both Holmes and Chivers; it also appeared in some of the women's results. To me this suggests that wearing the pheromones gave some of the test subjects an extra boost of confidence, which in turn made them more open and outgoing with potential romantic partners and people in general.

Chapter Seventeen

RUSSELL
The Deal Breaker Jeans

April 2005

IN MY LATE teens through early twenties, I worked in the restaurant industry as a cook. I was working in a five-star restaurant under a very famous chef; one night we were slammed, and I put an entree out with my greasy fingerprints on the plate rim. The chef saw it, looked me straight in the eye with such intensity, and said, "People eat with their eyes first." What a powerful statement. To this day, especially as such a visually oriented person, I live and practice that motto.

Russell and I are old friends from Venice. We used to meet for happy hour or bump into each other at the Canal Club, but we were always just friends. I never thought about dating him despite his cuteness; he was just the local guy I hung out with. About three years ago, Russell, who plans corporate parties and events for a living, moved to New York City. We've kept in touch by phone and email. He's a really solid guy and a good friend.

Recently, I was in New York on business, so Russell and I made plans to meet. I was really looking forward to seeing him after three years. We met for dinner at a noisy, dark, crowded restaurant. He looked just the way I remembered him: sandy blond/brown hair, brown eyes, about five-foot-nine and a nice body. He is a good-looking man. I had always wondered why he did not have a woman in his life.

I had seen other old friends on my trip to New York, and it was equally great to see Russell. We had a wonderful time catching up, filling in the details of our lives, laughing until my face hurt. He told me about his knee surgery, and I told him about the book; he shared New York war stories, I reminded him of all he was missing in Los Angeles—the beach, the Venice vibe, the smog. We talked about life and love.

After dinner, we decided to go back to the Mandarin Oriental, where I was staying, to have drinks. When we hit the street and the bright lights of Broadway (not to be cliché—we really were on Broadway), I noticed for the first time what he was wearing. They were the ugliest jeans I'd ever seen in my life. They were deal breaker jeans.

Russell and his jeans became like fingerprints on the dinner plate. As I stood there under the streetlights, I got a bad taste in my mouth. I thought, *Jennifer, step away from the jeans.*

Taste, of course, is subjective. He liked the jeans; he wanted to get lucky with me in those jeans. But as a great guy as Russell is, his pants were a major turn off: too tight, faded with a bleached-out swirl design down the legs, and bellbottoms. I think that vision will be branded into my memory forever, as much as I try to put it out of my mind when I think of dear, sweet Russell.

As we walked down Broadway, I began to think, *Can what a person wears be a deal breaker? I am not an unreasonable person. How could I judge a man by his clothing?* We had such a good time at dinner. Russell is a good friend, not to mention very attractive. He even told me that he had always had a crush on me. Interest was there, but could I overlook the jeans?

Walking down the street, we were quite the pair. I was feeling well put-together in a black Dolce and Gabbana dress and biker boots. Then there was lovely, kind Russell, walking with a noticeable limp from his recent knee surgery, in those dreadful pants. Shallow Jennifer was alive and well, walking down Broadway with a great guy in deal breaker jeans. I made a mental note not to touch them.

I asked to see his surgery scar, hoping it would take my mind off the bellbottoms. We stopped walking as he pulled up his pant leg to show me. The nasty, painful-looking scar on his knee only emphasized the hideousness of the jeans.

"Ouch! Looks like it hurts," I said, trying to focus on him.

"It does, but the doctor has me on good pain meds."

I had to look away.

Back at the Mandarin, we had a couple drinks at the bar, and then Russell suggested that we go back to my room. It was the first time he had been at the new hotel and was curious to see what the rooms looked like, or so he said. It seemed innocent. Since we were friends, I did not think much of him coming up with me. It was a beautiful room that overlooked the Hudson River—a picture postcard kind of view.

We sat on the plush chairs, looking out over the Hudson. It was a clear night; the reflection of the lights on the water was beautiful and very romantic. To my surprise, Russell leaned in and kissed me smack on the lips, tongue and all. Thoughts of the jeans crept into my mind, but the kiss felt good. The wine in my system was taking the edge off. I let myself relax: *We have history. He is sweet and I am in science project mode.*

We made our way to the unmade bed. The fabric softener the hotel's laundry service used made my skin itch the first night, so I had asked them not to change the sheets. We made out for a little while, something between PG-13 and R-rated snogging. It was nice, but the whole time I felt uncomfortable.

I told him I was getting tired and wanted to get to sleep. I asked him to leave, even though he asked to stay and spend the night with me. I gave him a good night peck on the cheek at the door.

In the morning, I noticed a big, brown dirt spot on the crisp, white duvet. Something from his shoes (or maybe from his jeans?) had gotten on the bed. I stood there for a moment with the spot—he'd left his mark, just like I had on that plate rim years ago. I felt like the chef was there in the room, pointing it out to me.

During the remainder of my stay, I laughed every time I saw the spot. I wanted to get the linens changed, but I didn't want to risk the potentially itchy fabric and another sleepless night. Russell called me several times before I returned to Los Angeles, leaving mushy messages on my voice mail. All I could see were the jeans and the spot, and I felt dirty.

Russell is a sincerely nice guy; I wish I could have that feeling for him, that I-can't-stop-thinking-about-you-I'll-fly-across-the-country-to-be-with-you feeling. But I don't. We stay in touch; he leaves me affectionate messages, sends kindhearted e-cards, and wonders when we can be together again. Russell is a man I consider a friend, but time, distance and jeans won't allow us to be more. I will always have a very special place in my heart for him but his deal breaker jeans are, at least for now, like smudged fingerprints on the dinner plate.

Chapter Eighteen

CHAD
Online Sex Wanted

May 2005

CHAD WAS THE first guy I met on Match.com who made it very clear from the get–go that he was online for sex: no strings, no games. This was completely new for me; I was intrigued, looking at the situation as potential fodder for the book. Chad was twenty-nine and just looking for adult, X-rated fun.

We had an email flirtation for about two months, and he always went straight to sex talk. I do give him credit for his honesty and straightforwardness. As a writer for the *Wall Street Journal*, he had a strong handle on the written word. Chad would try to engage me in "cyber-sex," but that is not my style. I like it in person. The whole experience was fascinating and kind of exciting.

In the exchange before we finally met in person, he asked what I was wearing. I told him. Then came the reply:

From: Chads_email@★★★★.com
awesome…underneath?

From: me@★★★★.com
Cosabella black g-string, no bra

From: Chads_email@★★★★.com
stunning! Any requests? Since I'm not dressed yet… unscented right?

From: me@**.com**
yes, unscented. I like to smell the man.
Gotta go, but
Are you hard yet?

(I was kidding...Well, sort of, kind of, maybe—this was all very new to me and he took the bait!)

From: Chads_email@**.com**
getting there...are you wet yet?

Wow. He was obviously very straight to the point. I was having dinner with a girlfriend that night, so Chad and I made plans to meet afterward for a drink at the Baja Cantina. I was satisfied with what I saw. He was a sexy brunette with brown eyes and a nice build. He looked even younger than his age. We had one cocktail. Though the chemistry wasn't completely overwhelming, there was enough to head back to my house without wasting time.

I felt safe with Chad; I was confident that he was not a mass murderer or a serial rapist. He was a good lover, and like Room #104, another man who seemed to watch porn. Not that I am an expert, but I have seen enough in my life that I can recognize requests that come from an aficionado.

I had on great four-inch heels—extremely rock 'n' roll—that I neglected to remove while we were making out on my couch. Coming up for air, he said, "Get up and walk around."

"What?"

"With your heels on, get up and walk around. I want to see you naked in your heels."

I was unsure if I should feel flattered. No one had ever asked me to prance around buck naked in my high heels. I was caught off guard. I did contemplate it for a moment, and then I said no with a giggle. The rejection didn't faze him. I asked him sarcastically, "Am I supposed to spank you, too?" We both laughed as he pulled me back down on top of him to finish what we had started.

The sex was just okay and we parted soon after. Chad, I think, felt more fulfilled than I did. For me it was an empty encounter, a moment in time I have no desire repeat. I was curious, and once that curiosity was satisfied, I knew with absolute certainty that cyber-sex is not my style. Neither are one-night stands with men I meet online.

Chad emailed me again for a hook-up about three months later, but I was not interested at all. My time with Chad was merely an investigation—another experiment in the science project.

Chapter Nineteen

Animals and Us

We are walking archives of ancestral wisdom.
—Helena Cronin, *The Ant and the Peacock*

WHATEVER YOUR STANCE on evolution, there is no denying our connection to the animal kingdom. The mere fact that humans are mammals illustrates this bond. While some of our most basic instincts may have become dulled by human progress, our cellular and genetic connection is still there, guiding us through life whether or not we realize or accept it. Every moment, we are faced with the realities of our link with nature and the thousands of creatures that share our world. Sometimes on my early morning run along the Pacific Ocean, I contemplate this relationship.

Huge waves created by hurricanes thousands of miles away crashed alongside me in recent months. I could feel the power of the sea and smell the salt and decay in the air. We are a part of the sea and it's a part of us. In her book *The Sea Around Us*, Rachel Carson explains that in the Precambrian period, over 4,500 million years ago, "When the animals went ashore, to take up life on land, they carried part of the sea in their bodies, a heritage which they passed onto their children and which even today links each land animal with its origins in the ancient sea. The sea within us has the same saltiness as the Precambrian seas of three billion years ago." Even human blood contains a water-to-salt ratio similar to that of the ocean.

Fast forward to the end of the Carboniferous period, 300 million years ago. Only a few insects had evolved enough to live out of water; early amphibious and reptilian creatures began to creep out of the oceans and rivers. These first vertebrates continued to develop and morph over time, creating millions of species, and eventually humans.

Humans have been on this planet for about four million years; one of the first and most notable pieces of evidence is "Lucy," the skeletal remains of a hominid called *Australopithecus afarensis*. Discovered in Hadar in Eastern Africa in 1973, by Donald C. Johanson and his student Tom Gray, Lucy to this day remains one of the most well preserved, early human skeletons ever uncovered. While the fossils indicated that she had short legs and long, dangly arms like our most closely linked cousin the chimpanzee, her pelvis and knee structure showed that she walked upright.[31]

We have come along way since Lucy. *Homo sapiens* arrived on the scene about 100,000 years ago, but modern humans still hold billions of years of cellular information passed on from our ancestors. There are some 300 trillion cells in each of our bodies. About ten million die and are replaced every second. And yet, our basic being still holds the history. Miraculous!

So how did we go from single-celled organisms swimming around in the Petri dish of the oceans to breathing, walking mammals? If we take a look out on the landscape of life, each being seems to have a mating ritual, but as strange as it sounds, all beings are connected in the end. Humans are programmed, just as many of our animal counterparts, for sex as a means of reproduction *and* emotional bonding.

Single-celled organisms reproduce by dividing, bumping up against each other. The more advanced the species, the more complex the reproductive process. "While some biologists have labeled humans the sexiest of animals, it is clear that there are few if any ways in which we are truly unique. Animal research often shows the close ties we have with our animal relatives and that there is rarely anything totally new in human or animal behavior."[32]

Apes and monkeys mate face to face, just like humans—a rarity among non-human primates. On the flip side, most insects mate lying in opposite directions, only maintaining genital contact. Porpoises engage in "group sex" with two males and one female participating.[33] Amazingly, some female chimpanzees have been documented having sex with eight different males in a span of fifteen minutes. Some have had up to eighty-four encounters in eight days with seven different partners.[34]

While it is somewhat uncommon in the animal kingdom, we certainly do not have a monopoly on monogamy. Lovebirds, wolves, beavers and swans are all known to mate for life. But monogamy in the animal world is a bit different than in ours. The main concern is the care and safety of the offspring; while many of these species live together for life, they do not often remain sexually one-partner creatures. Once babies are old enough to be self-sufficient, or only need one parent, even "monogamous" animals split up. A recent study of divorce rates in the U.S. showed that humans are beginning to follow that trend, with most couples surveyed separating when the youngest children are beginning school.

Animal Mating and the Senses

While the primary goal of reproduction is propagation of the species, it appears that even our animal friends are getting in on the sex-as-recreation trend. Of course, on a biological, instinctual level, all beings mate to generate new life. In *The Dance of Life,* Mark Jerome Walters explains this concept:

> Sperm are plentiful; eggs are a rare commodity. Consequently, male and female must employ radically different approaches to achieving their ultimate goal—to leave behind as many of their own descendants as possible. The female must be prudent in her investments. She must choose a male who will stir them to life with a fine and fit sperm, and who will remain around if necessary to protect the offspring. One way she can assure herself of a fit male is to engage suitors in a rigorous elimination heat, or courtship routine to winnow out the weak. Though personal taste may play a role, one seems to be inviolable: "Only the brave shall win the fair."

The human male regenerates millions of sperm cells every day. The human female has about 300,000 eggs when she begins menstruation; that number decreases to just a few hundred by menopause. So, why does it take 100 million sperm to fertilize one egg? Is it because none of them will stop and ask for directions? Well, maybe…but more likely, it's just some good, old-fashioned competition.

After ejaculation, millions of human sperm swim twenty-eight miles per hour through the vaginal canal and the cervix and into one of the fallopian tubes, in a fierce race to impregnate the female's egg. The strongest, more vital sperm fight the lesser to fertilize the egg. Once there is success, the egg becomes impenetrable. Similar examples occur within the animal kingdom: When honeybees mate, the male ejaculates and explodes, and as he falls to the ground, his genitals snap off inside the female so she cannot mate again.

The sperm, the smallest cell in a man's body, is responsible for penetrating a woman's largest cell, her egg. The more sperm he can produce, the more likely he will find success and carry on his line, ensuring his genetic survival. Interestingly, smell has been shown to play a role in all this as well. In a 2003 study published in *Science* magazine, researchers reported a discovery that sperm cells may have odor receptors that, when exposed to a substance called *bourgeonal*, make a beeline for the egg.[35] Conceivably, they don't need directions after all.

It may be a controversial statement, but I believe most animals have an edge on us when it comes to mating. They operate wholly from instinct, rather than from ego. A lion does not care what kind of car you drive or what kind of watch you wear. We have personal barriers, walls, static and fear that so often get in our way. But even in the animal kingdom, beauty plays a part.

Darwin illustrates this in *The Origin of the Species*, in his discussion of what he calls "Sexual Selection." Until the mid-nineteenth century, it was thought that survival was the sole purpose of mating and reproduction, but Darwin proposed that aesthetic traits were also a factor. Using the example of the peacock, he showed that while once there existed dull, plain colored males, only the most vibrant, brilliantly colored males were desired by peahens. Eventually the unimpressive peacocks died out.

"Beauty is a universal part of human experience," says Nancy Etcoff in *Survival of the Prettiest*. "It provokes pleasure, rivets attention, and impels actions that help ensure the survival of our genes. Our extreme sensitivity to beauty is hard-wired."[36] In *The Evolution of Desire*, David M. Buss concurs: "Our ancestors had access to two types of observable evidence of a woman's health and youth: features of physical appearance, such as full lips, clear skin, smooth skin, clear eyes, lustrous hair and good muscle tone; and features of behavior, such as a bouncy, youthful gait, an animated facial expression, and a high energy level.

These physical cues to youth and health, and hence reproductive capacity, constitute the ingredients of male standards of female beauty."[37]

But sight is not the only stimulant in the animal kingdom. We've already discussed pheromones and smell in previous chapters, but we must not overlook sound. While we have telephones, the Internet and other forms of technology, the main function of the mating call is for animals to communicate over long distances. The obvious example of attractive sounds is found in songbirds: in each species, the male has its own song to make the females flock.

However, many species of mammals also call out to mates. Tree frogs and humpback whales have elaborate, distinctive calls to seduce their mates. Using the example of the humpback whale, males compete for a female's attention by emitting complex series of sounds. Not only is the song's purpose seduction, but it also acts as an aquatic global positioning satellite, leading the female to his location. Crickets mate similarly. Male crickets rub their legs together, creating a rhythmic sound that entices the female. As the female sets out in search of the male, her walking mirrors the rhythms of the song pattern. Like the whale, the cricket's song acts as aphrodisiac and beacon.[38]

Touch is equally important in how we and other animals relate to one another. From inside the womb, we develop our first sense of intimate contact. We feel the warmth of our mother's body, and hear the vibrations of her voice and the sounds she encounters. Once out in the world, we search for the embrace of the womb, finding comfort in the feel of a cozy blanket and our mothers' arms. From the perspective of mating, we are drawn to touch someone to whom we are attracted, starting with hand holding and progressing to embracing, kissing and eventually to sex.

Some animal species depend on touch in the mating dance. The male American alligator rubs his body against the female, blowing bubbles against her face to comfort and arouse her. A female tarantula, through vibrations of the hairs on her body, senses the approach of a male, who then strokes her sternum with his leg to calm her before mating. Monkeys and other primates are very touchy-feely. The process of grooming one another is not only hygienic; it also aids in social bonding.

All of these sensory factors boil down to genes. Animals instinctually desire the strongest, most attractive mate they can get. We humans are also highly sensual beings. We rely on sound, sight, touch and smell to determine if a person is "right" for us. Taste is also a factor. Just like with our animal cousins, the goal is the breeding and survival of healthy children to carry on our genes.

Because of my medical history, I am something of an exception to that rule. I cannot have biological children due to complications from the removal of my right ovary at age thirty. Since then, I have never felt "my clock ticking." It gives me a wholly different perspective on men and mating; I look for different qualities. When I am attracted to a man, it is not an attempt to spread my genes or find a father for my "child." I am seeking an emotionally, intellectually, spiritually compatible partner. Being a great lover, as well as being easy on the eyes and smelling good, is a big plus, but I have never felt the need to marry just for the china.

One of my main criteria—and I am not alone in this—is the intelligence factor. Looks aside, what comes out of a person's mouth ranks very high on the attraction meter.

Recently, I spent a weekend in Las Vegas with a man I was very attracted to. We had spent a fair amount of time together before our late-summer getaway, but as the initial rush of physical and chemical attraction wore off, I began to notice more about his manner of speech and, more importantly, the things he said.

After seeing a great show, we went to Sensi, a very trendy, hip and swanky restaurant. During dinner, we chatted, enjoying the food and atmosphere. I looked across the table at him and noticed he was grinning goofily, looking around with the wide eyes of a ten-year-old. He picked up his fork, waved it around as if he were conducting an orchestra, jabbed it into his food and took a bite. Very slowly, he chewed and swallowed, his eyes rolling around then disappearing into his head as he said, "It's like a symphony in my mouth."

Suddenly, this handsome, sexy man had turned into a silly little boy. I sat there thunderstruck, debating whether or not to stick him with my fork. Lucky for him, I stuck it in my food instead. There was an amazing switch. I went from enamored to repulsed in an instant.

After that moment, everything he said was painfully annoying and insipid. I realized we just were not going to happen. No matter how handsome or well dressed, no matter how good he smelled, he lost his place at the head of the male pack. He is a nice man, and I wanted to give him anoth er chance—I was in Vegas after all. The next morning, I even had sex with him to see if he had the ability to overcome this situation. No dice!

After all this research, I wanted to know how this information played with others. So of course, I did a survey. Once again, my sample included men and women of varying ages, races, religions and economic and relationship statuses. My enthusiastic, very candid participants gave some surprising insights into human animal behavior.

My first question was about what first attracts them to somebody. Most men, 66%, responded that the face came first, especially the eyes and the smile. Age, body type, and perhaps surprisingly, boobs (a mere 12%) were down on the list. Women gravitated more to the eyes and mouth by a majority of 75%, and it was no surprise to me that smell charted with 60% of women as well.

Keeping with physical appearance, I asked my participants if they would still be attracted to someone whose style of dress they didn't care for. Only 33% of the men seemed interested in clothing, with one man responding, "No clothes is best." The women were split 50—50 on style, with just one woman adamant that the clothes make the man. Next, I offered a similar scenario with regards to specific body parts. Once again, 66% of the men said they could deal with one flaw (just one!) in a woman's body, while again, the women were split—53% to 47%. A shining example: "Tiny nose when I like big noses, sure [I can deal with that]. A cock like a soup can? Maybe not."

For the next set of questions, I asked my surveyees to rate on a scale of 1 to 10 the importance of the following criteria in a relationship:

Physical attractiveness

Men averaged 7.8

Women averaged 7.6

Sex

Men averaged 9

Women averaged 9

Communication

Men averaged 10

Women averaged 10

When asked if they preferred model good looks to intelligence and compatibility, the panel were 100% unanimously agreed that what goes on inside a person is hands down more important than what's happening on the outside.

Finally, the monogamy questions were not so simple. 75% of the men and 60% of the women said that they had cheated on a partner at least once in the past. So perhaps it's not shocking that 80% of the sample said no when I asked if they thought monogamy was possible. But their reasons were fascinating. A single, twenty-eight-year-old woman said, "I think mating for life is possible, but difficult and rare. People change so much over the years that a lot of times they become incompatible. I think that it is natural to have multiple partners over the years. But as far as monogamy is concerned, I believe it is totally possible and important within the lifetime of a relationship, whether a few months or a few years—especially when it comes to building trust and having a solid emotional foundation."

One of the men (single, age forty-five) agreed: "I feel too many people make their life-mate decision too early. One goes through many changes from twenty-five to thirty-five, and frequently these changes result in severe incompatibilities with their mate. Post-thirty-five, change is less aggressive. Life-mates should be healthy and fulfilling relationships. Long term trust and love are very important to me, and I believe they are key in longevity."

Based on the survey answers coupled with my endless research into human versus animal behavior, I believe that whatever our motivation or however we go about finding a partner in life, we all just want to experience a pure, human connection. It took a full year to complete this book. During that time, I saw seasons change, natural disasters on a biblical scale, man-made disasters, wars, death, birth, had my heart broken, and may have broken a few along the way. What I have come to realize is that the seasons connect us just like the oceans. The mysteries of the universe are equal to the mysteries of love. I think my grandmother was right about keeping some mystery in life. Mystery keeps us thinking—and living.

Chapter Twenty

THE WEEKENDER
Emotionally Available, Geographically Unavailable

June–July 2005

NO BULLSHIT, NO games: my encounter with The Weekender was an authentic, honest, unexpected moment, and so what I needed to happen. After two years with Simon, a physically and emotionally unavailable man, and my year of science, I had become a little disenchanted with the male population. Still I wondered why I was picking Mr. Unavailable and Mr. Fixer-Upper.

The night before a Fourth of July trip to Sedona, Arizona, I went to the Mercedes Grill for food and drinks. I was still feeling sad about Kevin and reflective about the past year and my past relationships. After I finished my dinner, I went for a walk on the Venice pier, and the June gloom was in full effect; a thick fog that matched my mood had closed in the coast. Up ahead was a surreal and uncommon sight. There were two people on the pier: a man fishing and a five or six-year-old girl on a bright pink Big Wheel with long, pink and white tassels hanging off the handlebars. As I walked by, she rode up next to me with adventure in her eyes.

"Do you want to go to the end of the pier?" I asked her.

She nodded enthusiastically.

"Is it okay if I take her to the end of the pier?" I asked her guardian. He said yes. Together she and I set off.

With a gigantic smile and much enthusiasm, her little legs pedaled as fast as they could go and the Big Wheel made its characteristic, engine-revving sound. She was picking up speed, but steering was still a challenge for her. She still didn't have a handle on eye-hand[39] coordination, and she kept racing toward the cement walls of the pier.

> "Don't hit the wall!" I shouted. She swerved, just missing it by inches, but making her way to the opposite wall. "Don't hit the wall!" I screamed again.

We went up and down the pier several times. As she veered and swerved, I screamed for her to watch out. I thought of Kevin. During our entire relationship, I was hitting the wall. How nice it would have been to have someone yelling at me, "Jennifer, don't hit the wall!" Now every time I walk or run down the pier, I think of that foggy night and the little girl on the pink Big Wheel. She reminds me to be mindful of the walls ahead.

When I left for Arizona the next morning, I was still upset over Kevin and what he had come to represent in my life, but determined to use my time in Arizona to move through my feelings. While I was at the resort, I woke up very early every morning for a long run under the hot, dry, summer desert sun. Surrounded by the high, red rocks and cliffs of northern Arizona, Boynton Canyon is considered a sacred place to the Apache, as it's the birthplace of their tribe. The canyon is filled with ancient cliff dwellings that were also inhabited by the Sinagua tribe.

I have been visiting the canyon for over five years; it's a place to which I feel a very strong connection. I knew it was a good place for me to shift not just my feelings from Kevin to healthier ideals, but also in my life and choices. For the first time in my life, I felt ready to have a real relationship.

Every morning on my run, I would stare at the sun, something I have always liked to do since I was a kid, no matter how bad it is for me. It's crazy but true—staring at the sun has always helped me change my perspective. It reminds me of the power we all have inside us. We are all made of the elements: earth, air, fire, water. Without the power of the sun or fire for survival, there would be no life on the planet.

Then one morning, I stopped myself. *I'm not going to go blind for this man or any other man for that matter. I have 20/20 vision. No man is worth ruining my eyesight.* I asked the universe to show me a sign that the connections that unite humanity are real, that a real connection with a man is possible, not just a fairy tale.

Back at the canyon resort in Sedona, I went to the library to check my email. There was a handsome Cree Indian from Alberta, Canada named RJ Joseph giving a talk about Indian history. I sat in the back of the room, listening as he shared words of wisdom from his elders. He told a story of a time when he was very low; I moved closer and sat down next to him. One of his elders said to him, "It's pretty hard to see the future if there are tears in your eyes."

I looked out the big north-facing windows at the red rock cliffs. Directly in front of me was a rock formation called "Kachina Woman." For Native Americans, this is the "Garden of Eden," the place where the first woman gave birth to the human race. Looking up at the site of ancient beginnings, I too felt I was starting again.

At the very end of his talk, he shared that during one of his own "rocky matters of the heart," his spiritual adviser told him, "We have to get it right with ourselves before we can get it right with others." It was as if staring at the sun had purified my thoughts, giving me the sign I had been asking for. I was moving into a place where I could see clearly again, making room for a better relationship.

I returned to LA on a Thursday, with a renewed outlook on love and men. On Friday, I went to the Mercedes Grill with a stack of pages from the manuscript and my iPod, ready to get some work done. As I shared a plate of sweet potato wontons with the bartender, the man next to me asked what I was working on. He saw the red pen and thought I was a schoolteacher grading papers. There was a powerful connection from the moment we exchanged hellos. I felt I could tell him anything. I even told him the Big Wheel story.

He was in town from Portland for the weekend to be a groomsman in his good friend's wedding. Every moment that we spent together that weekend felt true and honest: the sign I had been asking for. Only geographical distance stood between us.

Things started innocently enough: talking and laughing at the restaurant, walking on the beach, making out in the sand, taking half the beach (in our pockets, in our hair, in our mouths) back to my house—we left a noticeable trail of sand from my front door to the bedroom. There, in my bed, I discovered The Weekender has a perfect penis, which matched his perfect openness and honesty. Despite my cleanliness tendencies, I realized a little dirt is a lot of fun with the right man.

The three days I spent with The Weekender completely opened my heart, raising my perception to a new level. In just seventy-two hours, we became closer on human, spiritual and physical levels than Kevin and I did in eleven months, or

Simon and I did in two years—along with a lifetime of dating and relationships, The Weekender and I had a deep, intimate connection that transcended words. I was no longer sad; my perception had shifted. In every aspect but geography, The Weekender was the perfect martini mix.

Now I know it exists. My heart had opened to a whole new level of connection, and I knew what the possibility of love looked like. With this revelation in my life, I stayed in almost constant contact with The Weekender via phone, text message and email. After three weeks, I decided to fly to Portland to see him for another weekend. My last science project: Would he be just another male distraction or could there be something deeper and more profound?

With approximately 900 miles between us, I was not sure what to expect, but I was open to what life was presenting me. What if he was "the one?" Was I going to miss him because of mileage? There had been a lot of build up. Although I had no expectations, when I got off the airplane it felt right. The Weekender and I had another great weekend filled with open, honest conversations, great meals, clean air and sex connected to a higher place.

On Sunday morning, we sat talking and looking into each other's eyes over my egg white omelet and his eggs Benedict. We discussed my theory of why we met and the possibility of a future: Kevin had come to represent a lifetime of unhealthy relationship choices, from dirty skater boys to Mr. Fixer-Upper. My trip to Arizona had signaled a shift in my life and The Weekender was the sign I had asked for. Like Damon, he was another revelation that a truly available man was out there. He shared that he was going through something very similar. Somewhere along the path of life, we had both allowed our hearts to shut down.

Now there we were to help each other open up and move on.

> Looking even deeper into my eyes he asked: "Am I available?"
>
> "Emotionally, yes," I responded honestly, "but geographically, no."

He was exactly what I needed at that moment and nothing more. We still have a strong bond, and have some kind of communication almost daily. I care for him deeply, but I'm not racing to pack up my life and move to Portland. The Weekender taught me how to open my heart and my life for the right kind of relationship—the perfect martini mix. Now I know what it looks like, tastes like, sounds and smells like.

Chapter Twenty-One

Nature, Soul and Respect

When we think of the psyche, if we think about it at all, as a cousin to the brain and therefore something essentially internal. But ancient psychologists taught that our own souls are inseparable from the world's soul, and that both are found in all the many things that make up nature and culture.

—Thomas Moore, *Care of the Soul*

I WAS WORKING on the manuscript while having dinner at Typhoon, a chic, established restaurant (one of my regular haunts) in the Santa Monica airport. Sitting at the bar, I met a charming, smart and very handsome ninety-year-old man. He did not look a day over sixty. A retired flight instructor and pilot for American Airlines, Lou is still active in aviation, flying private jets. He also volunteers as a pilot for Angel Flight, a not-for-profit organization whose members use their own planes to transport patients in need of medical treatment at no cost to the patient.

I had just returned from a trip abroad; Lou and I talked about how much things have changed in the friendly skies. We discussed the apparent lack of respect people show fellow passengers and flight attendants—the skies are not so friendly anymore. Flying in the year 2005 has become more like a Greyhound Bus in the sky. People show up wearing pajama bottoms as pants and have to be told not to BYOB on the plane (this is against federal law and is not in compliance with FAA rules). Getting straight to the point, people can be downright disrespectful.

Lou told me that he and one of his peers often complain that the younger generations are "more selfish." They call them "The Me Generation." I told him about a very negative experience I had with a middle-aged man on a commuter flight back to Los Angeles.

The man was trying to fit his oversized carry-on bag into the overhead compartment, aggressively jamming it against my smaller, regulation-size bag. Over and over again, though it was obviously not going to fit, he kept smashing his bag into mine. Switching into Hall Monitor mode (my ex actually used to call me "the Hall Monitor"), I informed him that I had a glass cosmetic bottle in my carry on and asked him politely to stop. He said some pretty nasty stuff, and when the flight attendant came over to help, he angrily tried to turn the blame on me.

> "She has glass in her bag."
>
> "Yes, I do," I replied. "Your bag won't fit because I have glass in my bag?"
>
> It made no sense. Too bad I wasn't wearing an entire "Hall Monitor" uniform complete with a large, silver badge.

Lou was not surprised by my story. This is a man who has seen a lot during his ninety years on planet Earth. For a large portion of his life, he has been responsible for countless people's lives everyday in his career and volunteer work. His personal experience allows him to speak with truth about respect for others' lives as well as his own. He said, "The lack of respect has become more noticeable now because respect has disappeared."

Looking out on the sea of humanity, and on the verge of turning forty, I had been in deep contemplation with a theory I call the "Leaky Soul Syndrome." I believe that as people lose touch with their spiritual side, holes develop in their souls allowing basic respect, thoughtfulness and consideration for others to drip away. Sharing this with Lou, I asked if he thought people have a hard time with relationships because they have lost touch with their souls—perhaps even have "holes." He said, "Yes, people do seem like they have holes in their souls. If you do not have respect for others it cuts down on your own character and your own soul."

Then I told him a story about Larry, a man I had dated. We were having brunch on a beautiful Sunday at the Ritz-Carlton, in their elegant restaurant. As we walked around the buffet tables filling our plates, we stopped in front of the sushi station, where Larry proceeded to tell the chef how to make a California roll. In a true display of male ego gone unbearably wrong, he boasted about his own skills in the kitchen and his past experiences as a chef. I was mortified. After a minute, I left, unable to take his arrogance and lack of respect for the sushi chef.

When I got back to the table, he was already sitting down. His finger had a deep gash and was bleeding rather badly. He picked up a white napkin, wrapping it around his finger. I asked him what happened and if he was okay. He said that the crab leg he was eating somehow "cut" him. I found it hard to contain my judgment (or laughter), since California rolls are made from crabmeat. I could just see Larry self-righteously telling the sushi chef how to do his job, the chef getting annoyed and, whack! Had Larry's karma come back that fast or had he lost some of his soul connection? In my view, Larry's soul had holes that leaked all over the Ritz. Though the crab was dead in physical terms, I believe nature had reminded him that a lack of respect for others and a numb, careless existence is ultimately painful. Later he told me, "It is unbelievable, but my finger bled continually for three days straight."

I think that we all get subtle and not-so-subtle signs all

the time, but we have to listen and be willing to do the work to improve our lives.

As Lou and I sat at the bar sipping cocktails, discussing the life and soul connection, we were both in agreement that things in our modern society have changed. Where did respect go? Is the lack of respect connected with the loss of soul and the loss of connection with nature? As we go through life, can we develop Leaky Souls that leave trails of icky, sticky, gooey soul matter on others in our wake?

The bumps and bruises, the heartbreaks, losses and other rough life situations may make people hard and out of touch. It seems it has become easier for people to look outward rather than inward, seeking external bandages for problems instead of exploring an inner place where the answers lie. How do we evolve if we are not willing to go there? How can we have healthy relationships if we don't?

About a month ago, I asked a woman who lives across the alley not to put her trash into my trashcans. The amount of waste produced by her family's over consumption was making me crazy. I was sick and tired of looking at her life via the overflow of garbage week after week. When I very politely asked her not to use my trashcans anymore, she threw a hysterical fit. I could see the veins bulge in her neck. Her body grew tense as she yelled, "You are ruining the planet for my daughter!" The reality is that she and her family consume so much in a week, they do not have enough garbage space. Who is really "ruining the planet" for her daughter?

It became exceedingly symbolic to me. By not taking full responsibility for her own personal actions and behavior, it became okay for her to literally dump her trash on someone else and blame her own issues on another person. In the alley that afternoon, she got her leaky, sticky soul goo all over me.

Applying this concept to relationships and my twelve-month science project, I thought of Jill, my dry cleaner. Just how many of us have had our sweaters used like a towel? I decided to ask her.

I had just returned from Vegas with a man I had been dating. My carry-on bag was full of smoke-filled clothing—the perfect time to bring it up. Jill is always curious about my love life, so we had no problem discussing the situation. I asked her how many people bring in cum-stained clothing in a day and what the most common clothing articles are. She said that the person before me had given her just such an item. She gets at least ten people a day. She went on, "Mind you, this is just [what gets handed to] me, not the other people who work here. But when I see it I will always show it to a co-worker." I asked her if she'd noticed my cum-encrusted sweater when I'd brought it in, almost exactly a year before. She looked me square in the eye, nodding her head yes.

Was this humanity at its best or worst? I asked her if she felt like she needed to wear rubber gloves and a biohazard suit. She gave me another look squarely into my eyes and uttered an emphatic, "Yes!"

"There's this one man, a lawyer, who's in here all the time. Every time he hands me his pants it looks like he jacked on himself there is so much of it. And prom time is especially busy!" she told me. "I think that people don't care. I do think that people notice it, but just don't care. I see it on everything, but mostly on shirts, skirts, sweaters and pants."

So in the end what does this all really mean? We can analyze, study, over-think and have debates about stinky sperm, human connection, human chemistry, dating books, pheromones and love. We could spend a lifetime in deep contemplation about human existence and what exactly makes us all tick. Life gets thorny and complex, but I do not think it is rocket science. Really, it is simple. It all comes back to respect: respect for yourself, respect for others and a respect for nature—what we are made of.

> Your decision to evolve consciously through responsible choice contributes not only to your own evolution, but also to the evolution of all of those aspects of humanity in which you participate. It is not just you that is evolving through your decisions, but the entirety of humanity.
>
> —Gary Zukav, *The Seat of the Soul*

Chapter Twenty-Two

Twelve Men, Twelve Months

Life tells you nothing; it shows you everything.

—Richard Bach, *Messiah's Handbook*

AS I FLEW back from London, marking the big kick-off to my fortieth birthday, the sun shined brightly through the window shade. I thought about the past few years of my life, my ex-boyfriend and the twelve men I got to know while writing this book. Collectively, and each individually, they represented an attachment to an old belief system. I attracted non-committal men, and I was one hundred percent non-committal myself. Looking back on my entire relationship and dating history, I realized I have always gone for Mr. Unavailable, and in so many ways, I have been Ms. Unavailable. But not anymore.

There's nothing like traveling thousands of miles on your own to make you be honest with your thoughts and feelings. It became blindingly clear that I am now ready to let go of the old beliefs. The average life expectancy, according to the National Center for Health Statistics, is seventy-seven-point-six years, and I am more than half way there. Something about turning forty makes me want to start a whole new phase in life. For the first time, I feel ready for an available man.

Life is amazing. Just as my body and health issues have been my greatest teachers, so have the twelve men I dated during the past twelve months. I cherish and respect every one of them. Whether they know it or not, I am grateful. No regrets!

> It's a slow process, changing principles. And you'll never know they've changed until something that used to be right just doesn't feel that way any more.
>
> —Richard Bach, *Messiah's Handbook*

Simon

The ex! We are still great friends and keep in touch on a very regular basis. Simon holds a special place in my heart. He knows I am permanently here for him, and I know that he will continually have my back, too. While once I thought he was "the one," I know now that he is not. He was the beginning of my realization that I pick men who mirror my own behavior. He was never really available to me, as much as I believed he was. In the end, I love him and I know he loves me too.

Jesus

Jesus and I have kept in touch via email and text messaging. I have no desire to spend time with him or even hook up, despite the great sex. We email and text more infrequently as time goes by, and I am one hundred percent okay with that.

Room #104

I have no idea where he is, other than in a paintball magazine among my stack of research folders. Our last communication was in his hotel room. I had no expectations. It was exactly what it needed to be, nothing more, nothing less—a one-night fling.

Neighbor Peter

In an effort to be "polite" after not returning any of his phone calls, I responded to Peter briefly via email, hoping he would just go away. Most people get the hint. One day not long ago, as I was running on the treadmill at the gym, I smelled a strong cologne smell that I recognized. PePe Le Pew! I looked over at the treadmill next to me. It was him. Not sure what to do, I kept running, becoming even more focused on my iPod and exercise routine and using a white towel to shield my face. I have not heard from him since that day. Maybe he finally got the hint.

John

John and I have not had any contact since my phone blunder when I thought I was calling another John. Oops! Whether it was fate trying to push us back together or just a big brain fart, I am fine with the outcome. He is a kind man with his heart in the right place. I still think his Kar is cool. I hope he has had his teeth fixed and found love.

Dave

One afternoon while out doing errands, I ended up standing right beside Dave at a crosswalk on Main Street in Santa Monica. We were both surprised by our random street-corner meeting. It was somewhat tense at first, but ever since that day, we have kept in touch. We talk on the phone and email on a regular basis.

Not so long ago, we met at the Lobster for drinks. At the end of the night, we kissed. It was a passionate kiss between friends, although he wanted me to go back to his home. I said no—despite his sexy good looks and love of my vagina, lurking in the back of my mind was the ex-wife at the front door holding a bag of groceries, his clothes thrown all over the bedroom and the calcium-encrusted bathroom. I also pictured handing another embarrassing cum-stained sweater across the dry cleaner's counter. It was out of the question. Dave and I are now friends with no extra "benefits," and it will remain that way.

Kevin

On October 11, 2005, one month after our last email contact, I sent Kevin an email. It was a bold move (and a drunk one, I confess). I was feeling raw, but I figured it was better to follow my own advice and be honest. I told him that he had come to represent an old belief system that led me to attract non-committal men. My heart raced as I clicked "send" on the email. I honestly thought, *It's done. I just put the final nail in the Kevin coffin.* I even ended my email with, "Stay well."

The next morning I sat in front of my computer in a state of disbelief. There was a return email from him. It read, "Sounds good to me. If you want to get together sometime in the next week or so that'd be cool with me." *What?!* I said to myself. I responded with date suggestions and we made a plan for drinks. Then history repeated itself once again. In his typical Mr. Unavailable style, he cancelled.

I am cool with where we stand. We have established that we are friends. I learned a lot through my relationship with him. He was a Match.com guy and supposed to be my *Why Men Love Bitches* guy. Perhaps if I had followed the book, the outcome of our relationship would have been different. But I am glad I didn't. In the end, I think we both had the same *m.o.*, and my experiences with Kevin motivated me to change mine.

Scott

Even after a ten-plus-year history, when I thought about Scott, I drew a total blank, tracing three heavily inked asterisks by his name. As I continued to draw over them in a repetitive action, the asterisks became symbolic. Because of his high profile job, he has been hard to forget or ignore. There are constant reminders of him in the daily media. I do not want to be with him, but he reminds me of my own past decisions, and his lack of respect. It makes me think about my choices in men—my own repetitive nature. We do keep in touch on a very random basis, via email and text message. When I was conducting the surveys, I included him in the emails. He responded: "Lay it on me." He never got back to me on that. I am not surprised.

James

Not that long ago, at a mutual friend's party, James and I talked. It was amiable, but there were no sparks. He and I will always be friends, and will continue to see each other at social gatherings and parties. Later that night, after I left the party, he hooked up with a woman I know for a fact is not available. I realize he had been drinking, but I am glad I was not his choice of an unavailable woman.

Damon

It always brings a smile to my face when I listen to my voicemails and hear, "Hey, Shorty!" in Damon's deep, Midwestern voice. We keep in touch via phone, email and text message; we have in-depth talks about life, his dad's health status, work and our love lives. In December, I will be snowboarding and visiting friends in Steamboat, and I look forward to some face-to-face time with him.

Russell

Russell and I remain very good friends. In one of our last conversations, he made it very clear that he would like to take our friendship to another level, but with a 3,000-mile distance between us, and the vision of the jeans still strong in my memory, I do not see this happening. I also would be regressing back to my old ways in the quest of "the unavailable man." He is a good guy. I hope he finds a mate; I know how much he wants one.

Chad

After the last email, in which he asked for sex and I said no, I never heard from him again. It's okay. He was only part of my science project.

The Weekender

Since meeting and spending time with him, I have dated four men and had a fling with a Finnish man in London. The Weekender and I remain friends. I am thankful to have met him. I pick a different kind of man now, a seemingly available man—or at least one who lives within a reasonable driving distance. While none of the five men I have spent time with since are "the one," they are closer than anyone thus far.

The man I am currently dating sent me a text message the other day that said, "I want U," signed, "Me." Then for my fortieth birthday, he left a dozen roses in a beautiful vase on my doorstep. Looks like I am making progress.

> Every person, all the events of your life, are there because you have drawn them there. What you choose to do with them is up to you.
>
> —Richard Bach, *Messiah's Handbook*

December 2005

December 21, 2005 was just one of the recent high surf days to hit California. Pounding twenty-foot waves battered the coastline from north to south, damaging the Venice pier. It has been closed ever since.

The pier's closure has forced me to change my daily routine. This morning I took off my running shoes, turned on my iPod, briefly starred at the sun and set out for my inaugural two-hour walk along the Pacific Ocean.

The ocean was extremely cold but it felt good against my skin. At some point along the way, my toes even went a little numb, but it was something new in my schedule. After my beach stroll, I decided to keep my shoes off and walk the remaining four blocks home barefoot. The thought of trash, glass, dog poo, pee and other urban street hazards crossed my mind, but it felt like I was planting a new seed.

Having been fully vaccinated for all strains of hepatitis and tetanus, I felt confident as I walked, keeping an eye out for the possible dangers ahead. That afternoon I shed another old belief, created an opening and dropped another wall.

By the time I reached the front door, the soles of my feet were covered in tar and sand from the beach with an additional layer of black dirt from the city streets.

As I put my feet in the bathtub to wash them off, I thought of a quote by Ralph Waldo Emerson I had read when I was nineteen. While the wording might not be exact, the gist of it is: "Do that which you fear and your fear will die."

That quote changed my life and became a mantra. Twenty years later, while editing this book, another Emerson quote came across my desk: "All life is an experiment." I agree.

Bibliography

Books

Ackerman, Diane, A Natural History of The Senses. New York, NY: Random House, 1990.

Argov, Sherry, Why Men Love Bitches. Avon, MA: Adams Media Corporation, 2000.

Asimov, Isaac, Isaac Asimov's Guide to Earth and Space. New York, NY: Random House, 1991.

Bach, Richard, Messiah's Handbook. Charlottesville, VA: Hampton Roads Publishing Company, 2004.

Bajic, Erin and Lisa Purdum, The It's Just Lunch Guide To Dating In Los Angeles, 10 Finger Press (http://www.authorsteam.com/10fingerpress), 2004.

Behrendt, Greg and Liz Tuccillo, He's Just Not That Into You. New York, NY: Simon Spotlight Entertainment, 2004.

Buss, David M., The Evolution of Desire: Strategies of Human Mating. New York, NY: Basic Books, 1994.

Cabot, Tracy, How to Make a Man Fall in Love with You. New York, NY: Dell Publishing, 1984.

Carroll, E. Jean, Mr. Right, Right Now!: Man Catching Made Easy. New York, NY: HarperCollins Publishers, 2004.

Carson, Rachel, The Sea Around Us. Oxford, UK: Oxford University Press, 1950.

Chopra, Deepak, The Path to Love. New York, NY: Three Rivers Press, 1997.

Crenshaw, Theresa, The Alchemy of Love and Lust. New York, NY: Pocket Books, 1996.

Cronin, Helena, The Ant and the Peacock. Cambridge, UK: Press Syndicate of the University of Cambridge, 1991.

Dampier, William Cecil, A Shorter History of Science. Cambridge, UK: Cambridge at the University Press, 1944.

Darwin, Charles, The Origin of the Species. London, UK: J. Murray, 1859.

De Angelis, Barbara, The Real Rules: How to Find the Right Man for the Real You. New York, NY: Dell Publishing, 1997.

Fein, Ellen and Sherrie Schneider, The Rules. New York, NY: Warner Books, 1995.

Fisher, Helen E., Anatomy of Love. New York, NY: Henry Holt and Company LLC, 2004.

Fisher, Helen E., Why We Love. New York, NY: Ballantine Books, 1992.

Judson, Olivia, Dr. Tatiana's Sex Advice to All Creation. New York, NY: Henry Holt and Company LLC, 2002.

Kasl, Charlotte, Phd., If the Buddha Dated. New York, NY: Penguin Putnam, 1999.

Kasl, Davis, Charlotte, PhD., Women, Sex, and Addiction. New York, NY" Harper & Row, 1989.

Kerner, Ian, Be Honest—You're Not That Into Him Either: Raise Your Standards and Reach for the Love You Deserve. New York, NY: HarperCollins, 2005.

Kingman, Daphne Rose, The Book of Love. Berkley, CA: Conari Press, 2001.

Krishnamurti, J., Reflections on the Self, Ed. Raymond Martin. Chicago, IL: Open Court Publishing, 1997.

Louis, Ron and David Copeland, How to Succeed With Women. New York, NY: Reward Books, 1998.

Masterton, Graham, How to Drive Your Woman Wild in Bed. New York, NY: Signet, 1987.

Mason, Stephen F., A History of the Sciences. New York, NY: Collier Books, 1962.

Moore, Myreah and Jodie Gould, Date Like a Man. New York, NY: HarperCollins Publishers, 2000.

Moore, Thomas, Care of the Soul. New York, NY: HarperCollins Publishers, 1992.

Moptwane, Aman, The Power of Wisdom. Redondo Beach, CA: Prakash Press, 2000.

Morris, Desmond, Intimate Behavior. New York, NY: Doubleday, 1971.

Paget, Lou, How to Be a Great Lover. London, UK: Piatkus Books, 2000.

Peck, M. Scott, The Road Less Traveled. New York, NY: Touchstone, 1978.

Ryan, Robert E. PhD., The Strong Eye of Shamanism. Rochester, VT: Inner Traditions International, 1999.

Walters, Mark Jerome, The Dance of Life. New York, NY: Arbor House/W. Morrow, 1988.

Woodward Thomas, Katherine, Calling In the One. New York, NY: Three Rivers Press, 2004.

Zukav, Gary, The Seat of Soul. New York, NY: Fireside, 1989.

Articles (Web and Print)

BBC Staff. "Mother of Man." BBC, http://www.bbc.co.uk/sn/prehistoric_life/human/human_evolution/mother_of_man1.shtml, 2005.

BBC Staff. "The Science of Love." BBC, http://www.bbc.co.uk/science/hottopics/love/senses.shtml, November 18, 2004.

Block, Susan. "A Valentine's Greeting: Chemistry of Love." Counterpunch, http://www.counterpunch.org/block02122005.htm, February 12-13, 2005.

Condor, Bob. "A Chemistry Lesson for Lovers." Tides of Life, http://www.tidesoflife.com.

Cutler, Winnifred. "Our Pheromones and Sexuality." Athena Institute, http://www.athenainstitute.com/sciencelinks/pheromonesandsexuality.html, 2005.

Etcoff, Nancy. Excerpt from Survival of the Prettiest (New York, NY: Anchor Books, 1995), http://www.pbs.org/wgbh/evolution/sex/love/2.html, 2001.

Estep, Daniel, and Suzanne Hetts. "Sex in the Animal Kingdom." Rocky Mountain News, http://animalbehaviorassociates.com/pdf/RMN_sex_animal_kingdom.pdf, 2004.

Fisher, Helen. "The Brain in Love and Lust." McManWeb,http://www.mcmanweb.com/love_lust.com, June 26, 2004.

Psychology Today Staff. "Chemistry Lessons." Psychology Today, http://psychologytoday.com/articles/pto-20041123-000001.html, September/October 2004.

Ito, Shigeyuki. "Smell and Memory." Serendip, http://serendip.brynmawr.edu/bb/neuro/neuro00/web2/Ito.html, 2002.

Kane, Daniel. "Human Sperm May be Capable of Using 'Smell' to Find Egg." American Association for the Advancement of Science, http://www.aaas.org/news/releases/2003/0327sperm.shtml, March 27, 2003.

Keller, Helen. The World I Live In, excerpt reprinted by Ragged Edge Online, http://www.ragged-edge-mag.com/0901/0901ft3-2.htm, September 2001.

Kohl, James V., Michaela Atzmueller, Bernhard Fink and Karl Grammer. "Human Pheromones: Integrating Neuroendocrinology and Ethology." Neuroendocrinology Letters, Vol. 22, No. 5, http://www.nel.edu/22_5/NEL220501R01_Review.htm, August 6, 2001.

Mayell, Hillary. "Lovebirds and Love Darts: The Wild World of Mating." National Geographic News, February 13, 2004:

Mayell, Hillary., "Sex Tips for Animals: A Light-hearted Look at Mating." National Geographic, http://news.nationalgeographic.com/news/2002/09/0912_020912_animalsex.html, September 12, 2002.

McChristie, Pat. "Love and Being in Love: What Is Chemistry in Love Relationships?" Cyberparent, http://cyberparent.com/love/love-being-in-love-1.htm, 2006.

Muskin, Philip R., Anita H. Clayton, Helen E. Fisher and Serena Yuan Volpp. "Sex, Sexuality and Serotonin." http://www.medscape.com/viewprogram/3201, July 20, 2004.

Philips, Jennifer D. "Interview: Saving Whales." WhaleNet, http://whale.wheelock.edu/archives/ask01/0194.html, University of Hawaii at Manoa, 2001.

Psychology Today Staff. "Cupid's Comeuppance." Psychology Today, http://www.psychologytoday.com/articles/pto-20040921-000001.html, September/October 2004.

Sage, N.A. "Sternberg's Triangular Theory of Love: Illustrated (On-Line)." http://www.psy.pdx.edu/PsiCafe/Overheads/TriangularLove.htm, 2001.

Schaffer, Amanda. "Breath Analysis No Longer Just for Drunken Drivers." The New York Times, http://www.nytimes.com/2005/10/18/health/18brea.html?ex=1142744400&en=a0051b5f588da81b&ei=5070, October 18, 2005.

Simmons, G.L. The Illustrated Book of Sexual Records, http://www.world-sex-records.com, 1997.

Small, Meredith. "Nosing Out a Mate." Scientific American, http://www.athenainstitute.com/mediaarticles/scientificam.html, August 23, 1999.

Stanley, D. and J. Bedick. "Insect Mating Systems: Biochemical Mechanisms of Releasing Egg-Laying Behavior." Entomology 401/801—Insect Physiology Home Page, http://entomology.unl.edu/ent801/ent801home.html, 1997.

Other Internet Resources

Department of Energy, Office of Science: http://www.ornl.gov/sci/techresources/Human_Genome/project/hgp.shtml.

Free Dictionary: http://www.thefreedictionary.com/science.

Grow Seed: http://www.growseed.org/repro-paper.html.

Science Daily: http://wwwsciencedaily.com.

University of California—Berkley, Museum of Paleontology: http://www.ucmp.berkeley.edu/seedplants/seedplantsfr.html.

Wikipedia: http://www.wikipedia.org.

Footnotes

1. Robert E. Ryan, PhD, The Strong Eye of Shamanism (Rochester, VT: Inner Traditions International, 1999), p.2.

2. Wikipedia.org. S.v. "science." Retrieved November 2005 from http://wwwencyclopedia.thefreedictionary.com/science.

3. Shigeyuki Ito, "Smell and Memory," Serendip, http://serendip.brynmawr.edu/bb/neuro/neuro00/web2/Ito.html, 2002.

4. Amanda Schaffer, "Breath Analysis No Longer Just for Drunken Drivers," The New York Times, http://www.nytimes.com/2005/10/18/health/18brea.html?ex=1142744400&en=a0051b5f588da81b&ei=5070, October 18, 2005.

5. Helen Fisher, PhD, Anatomy of Love (New York, NY: Henry Holt and Company LLC, 2004), p.41.

6. Helen Keller, The World I Live In, excerpt reprinted by Ragged Edge Online, http://www.ragged-edge-mag.com/0901/0901ft3-2.htm, September 2001.

7. Fisher, Anatomy of Love, p.43.

8. Psychology Today Staff, "Cupid's Comeuppance," Psychology Today, http://www.psychologytoday.com/articles/pto-20040921-000001.html, September/October 2004.

9. Fisher, Anatomy of Love, pp.40-41.

10. Charlotte Kasl, PhD, If the Buddha Dated (New York, NY: Putnam Penguin, 1999), pp.83, 84.

11. Susan Block, PhD, "A Valentine's Greeting: Chemistry of Love," Counterpunch, http://counterpunch.org/block02122005.html, February 12-13, 2005.

12. Helen Fisher, PhD. and Psychology Today Staff, "Cupid's Comeuppance," Psychology Today, http://www.psychology-today.com/articles/pto-20040921-000001.html, September/October 2004.

13. Fisher, Anatomy of Love, p.52.

14. Helen Fisher, PhD, "The Brain in Love and Lust," Mcmanweb.com, http://www.mcmanweb.com/love_lust.htm, June 26, 2004.

15. Helen Fisher, PhD, Why We Love (New York, NY: Ballantine Books, 1992), p.89.

16. Ibid., p. 182.

17. Fisher, "The Brain In Love and Lust," McManweb.com, http://www.mcmanweb.com/love_lust.htm, June 26,2004.

18. Fisher, Anatomy of Love, p.53.

19. Psychology Today Staff, "Cupid's Comeuppance," http://www.psychologytoday.com/articles/pto-3512.html, September/October 2004.

20. Pat McChristie, "Love and Being In Love: What Is Chemistry in Love Relationships?" Cyberparent.com, http://www.cyberparent.com/love/love-being-in-love-1.htm, 2006.

21. Bob Condor, "A Chemistry Lesson for Lovers," Tidesoflife.com, http://www.tidesoflife.com/chemistry-lessonforlovers.htm February 9, 2000.

22. Fisher, Why We Love, p.94.

23. N.A. Sage, "Sternberg's Triangular Theory of Love: Illustrated (On-Line)," http://www.psy.pdx.edu/PsiCafe/Overheads/TriangularLove.htm, 2001.

24. Fisher, Why We Love, p.91.

25. Fisher, Anatomy of Love, p.165.

26. Winnifred Cutler, PhD, "Our Pheromones and Sexuality," AthenaInstitute.com, http://www.athenainstitute.com/sciencelinks/pheromonesandsexuality.html, 2005.

27. BBC Staff, "The Science of Love," BBC, http://www.bbc.co.uk/science/hottopics/love/senses.shtml, November 18, 2004.

28. Meredith F. Small, "Nosing Out a Mate," Scientific American, http://www.athenainstitute.com/mediaarticles/scientificam.html, August 23, 1999.

29. Mark Jerome Walters, The Dance of Life (New York, NY: Arbor House, 1988), p.90.

30. Cutler, "Our Pheromones and Sexuality."

31 BBC Staff, "Mother of Man," BBC, http://www.bbc.co.uk/sn/prehistoric_life/human/human_evolution/mother_of_man1.shtml, 2005.

32. Daniel Estep, PhD and Suzanne Hetts, PhD, "Sex in the Animal Kingdom," Rocky Mountain News, http://animalbehaviorassociates.com/pdf/RMN_sex_animal_kingdom.pdf, 2004.

33. GL Simmons, The Illustrated Book of Sexual Records, http://www.world-sex-records.com, 1997.

34. Olivia Judson, quoted by Hillary Mayall in "Sex Tips for Animals: A Light-hearted Look at Mating, "National Geographic, http://news.nationalgeographic.com/news/2002/09/0912_020912_animalsex.html, September 12, 2002.

35. Daniel Kane, "Human Sperm May be Capable Of Using 'Smell' to Find Egg," American Association for the Advancement of Science, http://www.aaas.org/news/releases/2003/0327sperm.shtml, March 27, 2003.

36. Etcoff, Nancy, excerpt from Survival of the Prettiest (New York, NY: Anchor Books, 1995), found on http://www.pbs.org/wgbh/evolution/sex/love/2.html.

37. David M. Buss, The Evolution of Desire: Strategies of Human Mating (New York, NY: Basic Books, 1994), p.53.

38. D. Stanley and J. Bedick, "Insect Mating Systems: Biochemical Mechanisms of Releasing Egg-Laying Behavior," http://entomology.unl.edu/ent801/mating.html,1997.

39. I believe the phrase "hand-eye coordination" is misleading; our eyes see and then our hands react.